The Tarot Book of Love

The Ultimate Guide to Your Big Relationship Questions

Amira Sloane

Wandering Bobcat Books LLC

Copyright

♥

phrase any part, or the content within this book, without the consent of the author or publisher.

Disclaimer Notice:

Please note the information contained within this document is for educational and entertainment purposes only. All effort has been executed to present accurate, up to date, reliable, complete information. No warranties of any kind are declared or implied. Readers acknowledge that the author is not engaged in the rendering of legal, financial, medical or professional advice. The content within this book has been derived from various sources. Please consult a licensed professional before attempting any techniques outlined in this book.

By reading this document, the reader agrees that under no circumstances is the author responsible for any losses, direct or indirect, that are incurred as a result of the use of the information contained within this document, including, but not limited to, errors, omissions, or inaccuracies.

I have a gift for you.

♥

First things first, I know newer Tarot readers struggle to keep the meanings straight as they get started. I, therefore, made a printable card meaning reference guide to have handy. I made one that is more general in nature, so it can be used across all sorts of readings. It will hopefully help you get your answers more quickly.

Download a printable card meaning reference guide by visiting this link: https://bit.ly/AmiraS

The Tarot Book of Love

Printable Card Meanings

General Meanings For Any Reading

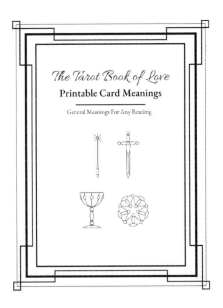

Contents

Introduction: Why a love book?

♥

Kelly is a single woman working as an administrative assistant in an office with a group of people that she really likes. Her co-worker Steve is someone she especially has a lot in common with. He's a runner like her, he has a cute golden retriever named Sammy (Kelly is a dog person, too), and they both come from the Midwest and have stories to share about how they grew up. She can't help but think he's cute, and he seems to like her too, but how much? Should she invite him out to dinner and a movie sometime? If things get weird, that could make life at work uncomfortable. What did he mean when he said he really hoped she'd come to the happy hour everyone was invited to at the end of the week? It is so hard to put yourself out there, but wouldn't it be nice to have someone in her life like this?

Or meet Alice and Michael. After meeting at a mutual friend's birthday party, they have been dating for three years and live together. Alice would like to get married, but Michael seems reluctant to commit. She wants to stay home and hang out, while he likes to go out with friends a few times a week. What does he do when he's out with his friends? He insists it's just innocent fun, but Alice isn't so sure. Is she just being needlessly suspicious? Her last boyfriend cheated on her, and it's hard to trust. Is Michael "the one" or not? How can she get him to settle down and think long-term with her?

And then there's Maggie and April, who split up after about a year of dating. Maggie is enjoying being single again and is eager to take time to just be by herself and heal. April is having a harder time and calls, texts, and invents reasons to get together. She says it's just to try to be friends post-break-up, but it feels a little manipulative. Maggie does care about her and hates to see her suffer, but she also wants the chance to be by herself and see what else life has to offer, so what can she do? This is over, right?

Relationships can be challenging, but your Tarot cards are there to help you navigate through it. They are the non-biased third party, there to dish out some tough love with the very best of intentions. They can guide you and help you to look at things from all angles before making decisions. The greatest thing in life is to love and be loved, but the pathway through it isn't always so straightforward. You don't have to go it alone, and this book is here to guide you through how to get the most seamless readings for your big love questions.

I first became interested in the Tarot back in high school when I pooled my babysitting money together, rode my bike down to the nearby metaphysical shop, and bought my first deck of cards. They were beautiful, and I was fascinated by the thought of these cards guiding me or telling me about my future. I clearly had a lot to learn, but it kicked off a lifelong journey of studying and using my cards, enjoying the value it would add to myself and others.

The most common questions that I field in my readings are about love. It especially pulls at my heartstrings when

I hear of someone at home with a Tarot deck trying and failing to decipher their cards over their big love questions on their own. It isn't easy to translate the traditional meanings into ones targeted toward love and relationships. Not everyone can afford to have a professional reading done every time life has a hiccup or some may be nervous about doing it in the first place for various reasons. It feels much safer to try it quietly on your own, ordering a deck of cards online and then seeing what you get when you deal them out. I want you to be successful at this. And honestly, if I can learn to do it, so can you, with a bit of practice, study, and patience.

First, I will share some tips to set yourself up for a productive reading. Then, I have included love meanings for each of the cards, to help you answer your big love questions. Finally, I have included some different card spread options, to fit the question you are asking. With all three in place, you will be well set up to get the answers you have been looking for from your cards. What do you say? Let's get going!

Chapter 1: Before you look up a card meaning, do a few things first.

♥

How many times has this happened to you? You've got a question on your heart and need some input. So, you grab your go-to Tarot deck. You shuffle the cards and lay them out for a reading. You look at what you got, and none of it makes any sense whatsoever. You look in your book or your notes, and what it says doesn't fit your situation at all. It's frustrating, isn't it?

I've assembled some tips to help you head that off and set yourself up for success. There are many ideas on how to break through that block, but this is what I found to be most helpful over the years.

Set the scene.

I don't know about you, but my readings never work well when pulling cards in a chaotic environment. It always seems like my most important life questions hit me when I have to be somewhere soon, and I am not quite put together yet. I sit down really quick to do it, and the dog starts barking at the delivery guy that just showed up. Then a family member comes to me needing help with something. Ugh, I just need a minute to myself to look at this! Do you know what I mean? Tarot readings work best when our hearts, minds, and environments are clear and we have made the space to do it right. It is always better to take note of your question and do it later in those circumstances.

Consider the place where you pull your cards. Do you have table space available to spread your cards out? Do you want to grab your favorite crystals or a candle to make it feel more comfortable? I have a card mat that I sewed for my readings (and there are some cute ones on Etsy, too), so I can be sure I have a big enough and clear enough space for it. It allows you to see all your cards well. If I can't fold it out fully, I have not allowed myself enough room to do my reading.

Is your head clear? What do you need to do to set your to-do list aside mentally? Maybe you block off the next 30 minutes to do nothing but your Tarot reading, so you can focus on your cards. You can set a timer so there's a clear boundary between your Tarot time and your to-do list. The clarity that comes from a good Tarot reading can make you feel more focused on your to-do list later when you pick it back up. Take the time for yourself to explore what's on your heart and your mind.

What about emotional clarity? This can be a tougher one. It can be hard to get clarity from your reading for issues you are emotionally involved in. It would be best to try to get your emotions to a more neutral place before pulling the cards. I find meditation to be a great way to do that. Taking the time and space to breathe and take the heat out of your feelings will lead to a better reading. I personally like to use a meditation app on my phone, but there are lots of guided meditations to be found for free online if you need some help getting to a more relaxed frame of mind.

Some Tarot readers have rituals around when they begin or close a reading. They have actions they take, like a particular candle, a special prayer, or an intention-setting exercise that mentally and emotionally prepares them. There is no right or wrong way to do it, though you will get better results if you take care to evaluate your environment and yourself before you begin.

Don't rely exclusively on what the traditional card meanings say.

That's funny, coming from a card-meaning-focused book, but this is probably my favorite piece of advice someone gave me when I was first learning to do Tarot readings years ago. Your intuition about the cards plays a part, and you do yourself a disservice by not taking a beat to see what your gut tells you when you first look at them.

As you probably remember, in school, you used rote memorization a lot to remember what you were learning. You probably memorized spelling words that way, history facts, the steps to certain math problems, and more. While having a basic understanding of the core message of each card is important, you also need to learn to listen to your initial impression of what you're seeing as well.

Each of the cards tells a story. The Tarot is, at its heart, a language of symbols. You could be missing an important part of the message if you don't take a moment to ask yourself, "what are these pictures telling me?" and see how it matches up with your question.

- Which way are the characters facing in relation to the other cards?

- What symbols do you see in the background, and what do they mean?

- Are the people happy, sad, or stressed in the pictures?

- What are they doing in the picture?

- Is the overall color scheme light or dark?

For example, I was having a hard time getting along with someone. I got so frustrated that I turned to my cards for input. I pulled a card, and I got the Queen of Pentacles.

The card meaning is a creative, abundant, happy person, that is everybody's caretaker. The person I was asking about didn't feel like that to me at the moment! What struck me was the imagery. The Queen of Pentacles in the deck I was using is standing in the middle of an orchard, surrounded by baskets and baskets of fruit. I knew in an instant what the card was trying to tell me. The many baskets of fruit symbolized lots of work. I knew this person was up to their eyeballs in work, but I hadn't really focused on what that would be like for them. This card made me think about it, and I realized I needed to extend this person some empathy and understand that they had more than they could handle on their plate right now. That was the right piece of advice, and we got through it.

I realize there may be some purists out there whose feathers will get ruffled when it comes to deviating from the traditional meanings. But I believe we all have different personalities and life experiences that will naturally color the way we see and interpret the cards. Take the Hermit, for example. This is one of my favorite cards. I am an introvert, and the guidance to seek solitude is welcome when reading myself. I have friends and family, though, that are more extroverted, and therefore see the Hermit has a bad card to get when it comes up in a reading.

Once you have taken a beat to interpret the story in your cards in relation to your question, you can look to the traditional card meanings to complete the message. You need both – intuition and traditional meanings – to get the most out of your reading.

Pick your deck carefully.

Finally, since the artwork is so important, pick a deck with imagery that means something to you. There are literally thousands of beautiful options out there and incredibly creative ways that artists have designed cards to incorporate symbols and tell each card's story. Take some time, and have some fun exploring what's out there, and go with a deck and artistic style that speaks to you.

There is an old superstition that your deck is supposed to be gifted to you. I don't follow that line of thinking at all. As I said earlier, I bought my first deck (and several others since), and they have always worked fine for me. While it's nice for someone to give you some cards, no one knows what resonates for you better than you. Buy a deck you love.

Furthermore, own lots of decks! Even if you don't use them in a reading, it's wonderful to see how different artists interpret each card. It can also help clarify things when you get stuck. When your cards aren't making sense, you can do two things:

1. Pull another card to clarify what the original card was trying to tell you.

2. Or if your gut (intuition!) is telling you that card is especially important, but it isn't making sense, sometimes it helps to look at it in a different deck. Another artist's interpretation may include the elements you need to give you that "aha!" moment.

Keep a journal.

It is no fun to get a reading that doesn't make sense but remember that just because it doesn't make sense today doesn't mean it won't make sense tomorrow. Keep a journal of your readings, including the date of the reading, the question you asked, the cards you got, the impressions you got from it, and any other relevant notes. Come back to it down the road and see how it worked out. You'll be amazed at what didn't make sense back then, makes perfect sense now.

I have had readings (usually when I'm reading myself) where I ask the cards the same question multiple times, and the same cards keep coming up again and again. Clearly, there is a message there that I am supposed to get, but it just isn't making sense to me. Then, a little way down the road, the clarity comes. Aha! That's what I was supposed to get from it! I was too emotionally close to it to see it initially, but I got it in the end. What a funny system the Tarot can be! I'm usually glad in the end that those cards kept coming up.

Chapter 2: First, some basics about the cards.

♥

Your deck is made up of seventy-eight cards, organized into two chunks. The first chunk is the Major Arcana, which represents the main life moments you will experience. It follows the story of the Fool, as he/she moves through the journey of life. The Fool is card number zero, and represents the beginning of something. There are twenty-one life moments that happen thereafter. The Fool manifests what they want via the Magician card. They then fall in love with the Lovers card. They get stuck in an uncomfortable spot with the Hanged Man card. Life comes apart with the Tower card. Everything comes together in a happy way in the end with the World card. There are many other cards in between, but you get a general idea. Note that in life, we will have many moments where we cycle through the story of the Fool. You start a new job or a new relationship, and in those moments, you are the Fool. You reach the completion of those experiences with the last card, the World. And then the journey begins again.

The next fifty-six cards in the deck are called the Minor Arcana and are organized somewhat like what you'd recognize in a Las Vegas style deck of playing cards. There are four suits of cards. Rather than diamonds, hearts, clubs, or spades, we have cups, swords, pentacles (or coins, depending on the artist), and wands (or rods, depending on the artist.) The cards are numbered starting with the ace, then two, three, four, on up to ten cards. Then, there are also the page, knight, queen and king of each suit as well.

The Minor Arcana cards represent more of the day-to-day issues, challenges and successes that we face. It isn't that they are less important than the Major Arcana cards, but it is clever that it is broken up this way. Is the issue you are facing a major life ordeal? Or something that feels huge in the moment, but it maybe isn't as important in the broader scheme of things? It is nice to get that perspective. And, it's nice to have guidance on both!

Here's a quick guide to each suit of the Minor Arcana:

- **Cups** – represent the water element. Cups cards focus more on emotions and feelings, how you relate to others, love and relationships, and creative pursuits.

- **Swords** – represent the air element. Swords are more about logic, making decisions, and anything to do with the mind.

- **Pentacles (or Coins)** - represent the earth element. Pentacles cards focus on your work, your money, and getting what you want and need out of life.

- **Wands (or Rods)** - represent the fire element. Wands cards are about the actions you take in life, your passions, achievements, and new ideas.

A quick note about reversals.

What is a reversal? Plain and simple, it's when you draw a card from your deck, and it comes out upside down. It has a different meaning when it comes out that way, though some follow that rule, and some don't. It is up to you. If you are a newbie at the Tarot, I would suggest just reading them all in their upright orientation until you know the cards better, and then you can add on looking at it with reversals included down the road when you're more confident.

When a card comes out reversed, it usually takes the opposite meaning from when it comes out in its upright orientation. For example, if you draw the eight of swords upright, it represents feeling stuck or restricted in a situation. In its reverse, it means you will find a way out of what's making you feel stuck.

It is a lot to learn the meanings of seventy-eight cards as it is, so again, if you are newer, just stick with upright meanings for now. For those a little further into their Tarot journey, I will also include the reverse meanings so that you can see it both ways.

Chapter 3: The Major Arcana

♥

The Fool

♥

Every journey begins with a single step, just as every relationship starts with a leap of faith. You never know how it's going to turn out until you take the plunge. Is this person right for me? Should I think this over? Should I throw myself into it with all my heart? The Fool will help you figure it out.

Common Portrayal

The Fool sets out on the journey of a lifetime, possessions slung over one shoulder. An abyss yawns at the Fool's feet while their dog yaps a warning.

The Card Upright

The message of the Fool card seems obvious—watch your step!—but there's more than meets the eye. The Fool is carefree. They have all they need in their little pack. Life can't chain the Fool. The Fool has an open heart and mind. When considering a relationship—new or old—you need to keep your heart open, too. Look at your love life with fresh eyes.

Yes, you need to be careful (and listen to your pets if they tell you someone is wrong for you!) but you can't embrace love if your heart is full of doubt and worry. Examine those doubts with the open eyes of the Fool. Answer them with a free heart. And when love calls, go for it!

The Card Reversed

Reversed, the Fool's warnings come into full force. Firstly, the Fool is warning you to give your love life serious thought. The Fool reversed raises the question: *Are you ready for this*? Are you ready to begin a relationship with all the open-minded innocence of the Fool? The card won't tell you the answer here, either. It's telling you to ask the only person who knows. You.

The second warning is about other people. Sometimes, the Fool isn't you. It's the person you're interested in (or who is interested in you). Are they right for you? Are they taking blind steps of their own? We can sometimes commit to people who are unhealthy for us, after all. The card warns you to make sure you aren't letting a Fool into your life who will take you off that cliff with them.

Affirmation

I will follow my heart. I am open and ready to let it guide me.

The Magician

♥

A great love life takes willpower and determination. You have to set boundaries and make clear what you expect from people. Don't settle for second-best. Find a relationship that fulfills you. Easier said than done, right? Sometimes you just want to curl up and hide from the world and all its bruises. Well, the Magician is here to show you the way forward.

Common Portrayal

One arm raised to the heavens, surrounded by symbols of power, the elements, and eternity, the Magician manifests their will and shapes the world accordingly.

The Card Upright

When the Magician enters your Tarot reading, it's time to make your dreams come true. You aren't the Fool anymore, discovering the world with wide eyes. You know what you want from a relationship. This card is about getting it. Think about the classic magician. By spell, prayer, incantation, or ritual, the magician changes the world through an act of will. Now it's your turn.

It's all about focus. Envision what you need from yourself and your partner to make your relationship work, then manifest it yourself. Think of all the things that make you unique. Your personality. Your passions. Your experiences. Focus on them. Lean into them to create the outcome you want. Just like the Magician on the card, you're surrounded by your tools of power. Use them.

The Card Reversed

When reversed, the Magician is a reminder to stay focused. It can be hard to set boundaries in relationships and painful to let go of someone, even when it's the right thing to do. The Magician reversed reminds you to keep your head about you and listen to your intuition. Deep down, you'll know when you're making a mistake. The Magician can help you remember that.

The Magician can also be a warning that you're straying from your true path. Sometimes we can get caught up in our desires and let them take us over. Or we can get hung up on that one special person, even when they're bad for us. The Magician tells us to stop and assess. Are you sure you're where you should be?

Affirmation

I know what I want. I will use all my powers to achieve it.

The High Priestess

♥

Sometimes you know the answer to a question before you ask it or have a feeling about someone that turns out to be accurate. That's your intuition talking, and you've probably learned to listen to it. We all have powerful subconscious senses that can spot subtle signs and signals. The High Priestess is here to help you tap into those inner insights.

Common Portrayal

The High Priestess sits at the entrance to the temple, its pillars adorned with sacred runes of power. The entrance to the temple is veiled, the priestess granting access to only a few.

The Card Upright

The High Priestess tells us to trust our instincts. She's like a Magician who has learned to listen to that quiet voice within, telling her how to best use her powers. When the High Priestess appears in your reading, she's telling you the same thing. Let the clamor of your thoughts be still for a while. Find a quiet spot. Meditate if you like. Or just chill and listen to what your gut is telling you.

More than that, the High Priestess represents a call to compassion and empathy. These are the cornerstones of every relationship—doubly so when love is involved. The card is a reminder to put yourself in the other person's shoes. What might they be feeling or going through right now? Ask yourself how you would feel if you were in the same situation and use this to guide your response. This unspoken insight is the most powerful aspect of this card, and you'll see real results if you live by it.

The Card Reversed

When the High Priestess appears reversed, it's a reminder to stop and take stock of your inner life. Is it in balance with the rest of your world? Intuition is a powerful tool, but don't abandon reason. You must master both to have a successful love life. Don't let yourself be drawn into fantasies that can never come true. Dreams are wonderful but you have to live in the world.

Sometimes, of course, you're not the problem. The High Priestess guards the veil that keeps the unworthy out of the temple and when reversed, she's your own personal love life guardian. Are there people in your life who are super gossipy, share secrets they shouldn't, or who lurch from one overly dramatic scenario to another? These people can drag you into their dramas and the High Priestess is telling you to take care around them. Remember: it's all about balance.

Affirmation

I will trust my intuition. I will find balance.

The Empress

♥

Life is for living, and love is for loving. We all face our struggles and sometimes they seem overwhelming. That's when we need someone to reach out and remind us it's going to be OK. The Empress does just that. She's loving, maternal, and powerful and she's going to lift you up and show you how to enjoy life!

Common Portrayal

Clad in finery, crowned with stars, the Empress reclines fulfilled. Around her, nature spreads in all its glory.

The Card Upright

The Empress is here, and it's time to live a little! She's learned the secrets of intuition at the High Priestess' temple and emerged full of life and happy in her own skin.

She's telling you to embrace your sensuality, enjoy your body (and your partner's!) and take time to savor the good things in life. With love and care and respect for yourself, go ahead and indulge in some good times. Don't be so anxious—the Universe is watching out for you.

And that's the other main aspect of this card—caring. The Empress isn't just about big time sensuality. She's about watching over the people in her care. You can embody this in your own relationships, too. Think of the people in your life. Is there a way you can support them? What can you do that will help your loved ones enjoy the good things in their own life?

The Card Reversed

When reversed, the Empress is a reminder to love yourself. Some relationships—some *affairs*—are so overwhelming that we lose ourselves in them. This can hurt you or those you love. The Empress reversed tells you to ease off the gas and make sure you're doing what's healthy for you. Learn to be your own Empress, always looking out for your own best interests.

More specifically, the Empress tells you not to be too critical of your flaws. We all have them. Don't hate your body. It's good to live a healthy life and strive to have a healthy figure, but let's be realistic—the world is a hard place, and you can't hit every goal. That's OK. You can be kind to yourself. It's what the Empress would want for you.

Affirmation

I am beautiful and powerful. I will love the life I live.

The Emperor

♥

When you're right, you're right, and you know it. You *feel* it. That feeling is an awareness of your own power, your own strength as a person. People can be weak and afraid, but we are also strong and able to overcome challenges that we never dared consider. When you're in tune with your inner strengths, you can accomplish the impossible. The Emperor is your mentor for the life you have always deserved.

Common Portrayal

Enthroned in majesty, the Emperor presides over his realm. He carries the emblems of his rank, sitting framed against an imposing mountainous landscape.

The Card Upright

The Emperor represents that part of you that knows what it wants, knows how to get it, and has a clear vision of what success looks like. You've learned from heartbreak and joy alike, and now you come into the fullness of your power. Don't settle for second best in love or life. Assert yourself. The Emperor is telling you to take what is yours. You're in control of your life. Don't let anyone take that power away from you.

An Emperor watches over his people and when this card appears in your reading, it may also be a suggestion to look at the needs of your loved ones. Sometimes, people need a defender. This card asks you to think about how you can protect those you care about. How can you safeguard their emotions and their needs? Unlike the Empress, this isn't just about caring and supporting—it's about making a stand for those who need it. A true Emperor serves the ones he rules by making sure they are safe. It's the same in our love lives—the people we care about are the ones who rule our hearts, and we should safeguard them in turn.

The Card Reversed

The warning of the Emperor reversed is one of humility. Relationships are seldom truly equal—the balance is always shifting. Sometimes it shifts in your favor and that's when you need to keep this card in mind, should it appear. The Emperor is reminding you to never take advantage of the power you might have over someone else, particularly someone you love. If this card speaks to you during a reading, take a moment to ask yourself whether you're treating those close to you as equals.

The Emperor reversed is also a warning to beware of others who might try to exert undue influence over you. The guy who won't take no for an answer. The boss who asks for too much. The relative who won't respect your boundaries. These are power imbalances. Protect yourself from them. Stand up to them if you can. Avoid them if you can't. Don't waste your time on people who abuse you.

Affirmation

I trust my power. By helping others, I help myself.

The Hierophant

♥

When you're feeling low or in need of advice, where do you turn? Your friends? Your family? Sometimes even complete strangers? Help and support appear in the most unexpected of places if you look for them. The Hierophant will show you how to find the support you need.

Common Portrayal

The Hierophant sits at the doors to the temple, robed and crowned. At his feet, people kneel, awaiting his wisdom.

The Card Upright

The Hierophant is a keeper of wisdom, but the wisdom of experience, not intuition. He's like an Emperor who has given up his throne to watch over his people. The Hierophant is a reminder that it's fine if you don't have all the answers. If you're struggling to make sense of your love life, ask for advice from someone who has been through life's ups and downs. And you don't have to be old to be wise—you can turn to a younger relative or friend for a fresh perspective. They might surprise you.

You can pay this forward as well. If this card appears in your reading at a time when you don't need someone else's advice, is there someone in your life who could use your insight? Can you use your own love life as a source of advice for someone else? Have you learned a few lessons on how to make the most of a relationship and what pitfalls to avoid? Maybe you can share some of your hard-won wisdom.

The Card Reversed

Let's talk about rebellion. When the Hierophant is reversed, it's time to rock the boat. As you'll have gathered, the Hierophant card is all about authority. Reversed, it's about *toppling* authority. Does an older relative keep putting you down? Remind them to get back in their lane. Is your partner calling all the shots? Step up and call a few of your own. We're surrounded by power structures. Go ahead. Smash a few.

The Hierophant reversed can also be a call to assert authority over yourself. Have you been part of something for so long that you don't even think about it anymore? A relationship? A friendship? An addiction? Do you feel like you've lost a little part of who you are? The Hierophant reversed is showing you the way back to self-respect. The only person who sets the rules for you is you.

Affirmation

I know when to ask for help. I know when to give it.

The Lovers

It's the dream, isn't it? That perfect someone. You're in sync with each other. Your interests align. Your passions enflame. Communication is almost telepathy. It doesn't have to be a dream. You really can find love, true and lasting. We wouldn't be here otherwise. But that love may not be where you expect it. The Lovers are about to share a few secrets.

Common Portrayal

Naked as the day they were born, the Lovers stand in an Edenic paradise. Above, an angel watches over them, sharing its blessings.

The Card Upright

It's exciting when the Lovers pop up in your reading, but it doesn't mean your soulmate is about to fall into your lap. The card is instead a kind of instruction manual (or wisdom learned at the feet of the Hierophant!) on how to be a version of yourself that's open to a fulfilling relationship, like. It's all about choices and communication. If you want to find that golden ticket, you're going to have to make some hard decisions and communicate your needs clearly. Exactly what do you want? No more mind games. The Lovers embrace honesty and openness. You'll have to do the same.

How? Here's the secret: The first person you need to be honest with is yourself. That's the deeper aspect of the Lovers card. Self-love. Yes, you can find true love even when you aren't happy with who you are, but is that the version of yourself you want to share? The Lovers card insists you ask yourself these tough questions. Have you been neglecting yourself or your own needs? Are you putting your concerns to one side in order to pursue your love life? You know that isn't healthy and the Lovers are here to remind you to love yourself first and foremost. It's the only way to be whole.

The Card Reversed

When the Lovers card appears reversed, it's a reminder to check that you aren't out of sync with the important people in your life. Have you been arguing more than normal with your partner? Are you finding it hard to make a real connection with that special someone? Ask yourself if you're listening properly to what they're saying. Not what you *think* they're saying, but what they actually mean. And if you aren't sure, ask them!

The card can also be a reminder to check in with yourself. We all have our personal beliefs and standards we try to live by. But desire can pull us off course. If you want to be the best version of yourself, the most honest version of yourself, you'll need to check your compass from time to time to make sure you're still headed in the right direction. The Lovers reversed is a reminder to double-check you're still headed where you want to go. If not, make a course correction by being open and honest.

Affirmation

I am ready to be the person I have longed to be. I am ready to share my true self.

The Chariot

♥

Relationships are like journeys (sometimes disappointingly short journeys!) and a successful journey demands good planning. It doesn't just demand it—a successful journey *rewards* good planning. When you've got it together, life is smoother and the journey all the more pleasant. Are you ready to take a ride in the Chariot? The open road is calling you...

Common Portrayal

A warrior rides a magnificent chariot drawn by mythical beasts. Clear-headed and adorned in might, the warrior guides the chariot through willpower alone.

The Card Upright

The Chariot is your vehicle to a better love life—but only when you're steering it. It's a powerful card and asks a great deal of you. You wouldn't set out on a long car journey without having some idea of where you're going or taking a few supplies, and the same applies to relationships. It's good to prepare. But sooner or later, you must act. If (like the harmonious couple on the Lovers card) you're in tune with yourself, your needs, and those of your loved ones, then do not delay in reaching for what you want in love.

So, the Chariot is a call to make sure you have your priorities straight when choosing a partner, but also to act decisively on those choices. That concept of moving forward is central to the Chariot. You can only put off acting on decisions about your love life for so long. Is there someone you have feelings for, but you haven't told them? What is holding you back? Do you need to make changes in your love life but are struggling to do so? Why are you procrastinating? Life will move on without you regardless, so take hold of the wheel and drive!

The Card Reversed

The Chariot reversed is a warning to stop and check yourself before committing to something big. Have you been properly open and honest with yourself about what you want from a relationship? Do you understand your loved ones' needs? The answer might be a simple yes, but the Chariot reversed will help you double-check.

The Chariot reversed can also serve as a reminder that you're the one driving, just like the Chariot upright. When reversed, though, it's specifically calling your attention to any obstacles in your way. Don't ignore them. You have what it takes to move forward but take care not to bulldoze everything in your path. Be a smart driver. Navigate the road ahead with a clear mind and open heart.

Affirmation

I put my life in order. I am ready for the new beginning.

Strength

♥

Confidence is a wonderful feeling. You're happy in your skin. You're pursuing goals that mean something to you. And then something comes along that knocks you off track. All of a sudden, that confidence vanishes, and you wonder what on Earth you were thinking. The Strength card is telling you to remember who you are. You can do this!

Common Portrayal

A woman strokes a lion, taming it with her inner power. Infinity itself is at her command—there's nothing she can't accomplish.

The Card Upright

True strength comes from within. It doesn't need to assert itself. It speaks and everyone listens. That's the kind of strength you need to cultivate. Like the driver of the Chariot, you know where you're going. State your truth simply. You don't need to control the people around you. Your quiet power will influence them. They might not even realize how strong you are. That doesn't matter. You know you're the one calling the shots.

Your strength doesn't just have to benefit you. Your friends and loved ones have needs as well, obstacles they must overcome, and sometimes they're just not up to it. If this card appears in your reading, ask yourself if you have what it takes to step up and lend your strengths to help those you care about. Maybe you can be present for someone in need, or maybe you just need to hold space for a person you care about deeply. You might be surprised at how strong you really are.

The Card Reversed

When reversed, the Strength card warns you to keep your power and influence in check, and your aggression and bad moods too! It's easy to underestimate the effect we have on the people close to us. An off-hand remark can cut deep. A decision you make can affect everyone around you. You're right to pursue your goals in love and life but be careful not to trample on those more vulnerable than you are.

The Strength card reversed can also be a warning light to check in on your own needs as well. Are you facing more obstacles in life than you expected? Take a moment to remind yourself of what you've accomplished. You're stronger than you imagined. Remember that. And if you're feeling low, your strength depleted, this card can be a caution to take the time to recharge before returning to the world again.

Affirmation

I am at peace in my own center. My strength is seen by all.

The Hermit

♥

Sometimes the world sucks, and so do all the people in it. That's how it feels, anyway. At times like that, there's nothing more tempting than to just hide yourself away until the storm blows over or until people everywhere stop being so horrible to each other. The Hermit thinks this is a great idea. That time alone is special, so don't waste it!

Common Portrayal

The Hermit walks alone, deep in thought, lighting the way with a single lamp. This is the only way forward.

The Card Upright

Sooner or later, we all need time away from the world to pause our journey and recharge our batteries. You might not realize you need a break, so when this card appears, use it as a prompt for a little wellness check. The key thing is to make use of the time you spend alone to assess yourself, care for yourself, and prepare for a return to the world. Don't forget—doing nothing is a valid choice as well.

In a relationship, the Hermit card raises some interesting questions when it appears in your reading. It can be a reminder to consider your inner lives as individuals. It's easy to lose yourself in another person and, while it can be wonderful, it can also be unhealthy. Make sure you and your special someone are giving enough time to your own interests, hobbies, and careers. When you both thrive as individuals, you're stronger as a couple.

The Card Reversed

When reversed, the Hermit is a perfect mirror of its up-right self. It's asking whether you're spending too much time alone when it might be healthier to get back into the world. This is the downside of taking an extended time-out—it can be difficult to call it quits. And we don't generally like difficult situations, so we avoid them. The Hermit reversed is a reminder to accept when the time has come to re-engage with the world and all its wonderful people.

Similarly, the reversed Hermit offers guidance when you're in a relationship (or just looking for one). Don't let yourself get too caught up in your own concerns—if you've committed to sharing your life with someone, that means sharing theirs just as much. When reversed, the Hermit is telling you to make sure you have the balance right between what you need and what your special someone needs. It can be tricky to find a shared space where you can be individuals together, so open and honest communication is important. Don't shut yourself off.

Affirmation

I embrace my solitude. I can end it when I choose.

Wheel of Fortune

♥

Change is the one constant in life. Nothing stays the same. That can be heartbreaking, but it can also be a relief. Unfortunately, we can't always control where that change comes from or where it will lead us. But there are ways to cope with that. Take a spin on the Wheel of Fortune and see what it has in store.

Common Portrayal

Inscribed with sacred text and flanked by supernatural entities, the Wheel of Fortune spins in the heavens.

The Card Upright

It might feel like you aren't in control of your life or your relationships. To one degree or another, you aren't. No one is—the world is too big and too complex. That doesn't have to be a bad thing. Like a wise Hermit who knows the score, you understand that the world keeps turning. In hard times, hold faith and know that change will come. In good times, make the most of what you have, for exactly the same reason. Nothing lasts forever.

The Wheel of Fortune isn't just about going with the flow, however, because we can control some parts of our lives—how we treat our loved ones, for example. The Wheel of Fortune symbolizes how the consequences of our actions will return to us. Treat those around you with love and kindness, and they will repay you with the same. You can call it karma if you like, but it's really just the basis of all relationships. Small deeds of compassion can cause a ripple effect through a whole community. The Wheel is a reminder that you can build your own good fortune.

The Card Reversed

When reversed, the Wheel of Fortune brings a warning. While many events are simply in the hands of fate, you aren't powerless. In fact, you might be responsible. When facing tough times in your love life or other relationships, it's worth taking a moment to ask how much your actions or behavior played a part. Be honest with yourself, even if it's difficult, and ask yourself what changes you might make to set the Wheel back on its proper course.

The Wheel of Fortune reversed can also be a suggestion to look for ways to change unhealthy patterns in your life. Do you feel like you're stuck in a negative cycle with a partner or other person? Or have you become stuck in a rut, making the same bad choices over and over? The Wheel is a reminder that the time comes for all things to change, and that includes you.

Affirmation

I will make the most of what life brings. I am ready to change.

Justice

♥

Someone is always judging you. Your family. Your partner. Your friends. Yourself. And that's as it should be. You have to be able to see yourself clearly. You have to understand how your actions affect not just yourself, but the people around you. It's a big responsibility, but the Justice card will help you meet it with your head held high.

Common Portrayal

Justice sits enthroned in a crown and robe. In one hand is a sword raised aloft, while in the other scales are held in balance.

The Card Upright

The Justice card is about accepting the consequences of what you have said and done. It's what always happens when the Wheel of Fortune stops spinning. You can't have a successful relationship of any kind if you don't take responsibility. And don't forget, Justice can be kind. You might find forgiveness or understanding where you weren't expecting it. Or you may have done a good thing without realizing it. When Justice appears in your reading, ask yourself if you've been shying away from owning your words and deeds.

Justice doesn't only apply to things we have done—it also applies to things we're going to do. If you have an important decision to make that can affect your loved ones, be sure to think it over. The Justice card tells you to take full account of how others might be affected by what you do. Be open and honest with yourself. Manifest compassion. When the Justice card next appears, you will know you did the right thing.

The Card Reversed

When reversed, the Justice card is asking you to be less judgmental, both of yourself and others. It's a warning to consider whether you're being too harsh with someone, or whether you're too critical of yourself. True justice grows from love, so you need to have kindness at the heart of any judgment you make. The Justice card reversed can be a nudge to take it easy on your loved ones and on yourself.

It can also speak to the world around you. Do you feel like you have been treated unfairly or unjustly? It's important to be able to accept criticisms from others, but when those criticisms and judgments are wrong, it's deeply hurtful. You don't have to take that in silence. You shouldn't because it only makes it worse in the long run, weakening your inner self-respect. Calmly and clearly speak your truth, and do not back down until you're being treated with the respect you deserve.

Affirmation

I do not fear the judgment of myself or others. I live an honest and compassionate life.

The Hanged Man

♥

It's easy to be overwhelmed by life and relationships, or the pace at which both seem to move. Often, you'll feel like you can't manage and that it's all too much. So maybe it is too much. So what? You don't have to understand and cope with everything. Sometimes you just have to be like the Hanged Man and accept life for what it is.

Common Portrayal

The Hanged Man is suspended upside down by one leg. His face is calm, a halo surrounding his head, as he contemplates life.

The Card Upright

You can't do everything. You can't solve every problem. No one can, and you have to recognize when something is beyond you. If you're struggling with your love life, the Hanged Man is a reminder to acknowledge your own limitations. Relax. It's okay if you can't cope. You don't have to. Take the time you need to find your inner calm and let life run its course. It will anyway, no matter what you do. This is as it should be.

The Hanged Man is a reminder to welcome these pauses. It's also a signal to change your perspective. According to ancient tradition, the Hanged Man is hanging there in order to gain wisdom—you can use the card to ask yourself whether you need to change how you look at your relationships. Is there another way to approach a problem in your love life? Seeking a fresh outlook can help you move past a problem that has had you stuck.

The Card Reversed

When reversed, the Hanged Man is telling you to stop bashing your head off a brick wall, stop, and accept your limitations—because trying to overcome some obstacles can be harmful. You might want to settle an argument once and for all, only to end up making it worse. You might stay up late to push through an assignment, only to find you made mistakes because you were exhausted.

In a relationship, this warning is even more powerful. You have to know when to call it quits. Often, we throw ourselves into a relationship with someone, knowing they aren't quite right for us but hoping we can fix them. Well, you can't. Not always. And trying to mend something that can't be mended will only wear you down. Is this what you really want? Sometimes, walking away is the only solution.

Affirmation

I let go. Life will unfold as it should.

Death

There's an old saying that every relationship ends in heart-break because somebody dies, or somebody leaves. What that saying is really talking about is change—all things change and so all things end, changing from one state into another. We shouldn't fear change and we shouldn't fear the Death card either. It's showing you the way to a new world.

Common Portrayal

Death's skeletal messenger rides his mount through the world. Beneath his black banner, nothing escapes his gaze.

The Card Upright

The Death card can be alarming when it appears in your reading, but you'll soon come to see it for what it is—a sign of changes on the horizon. Just like a Hanged Man who has learned from his meditations, you're now ready to move on to the next phase in your life. The Death card reminds you that everything runs its course, and you'll know when that time comes because you'll feel anxious and uncertain, but maybe also a little excited at the prospect of what's ahead.

This applies to friendships, relationships, your career, and your personal projects. Deep inside, you'll know when it's time for a change but maybe you can't take the plunge. The Death card tells you to feel that fear but do it anyway. There is power in taking that kind of leap and you will surprise everyone around you by showing your confidence and willingness to change as your life changes.

The Card Reversed

Death reversed is a sharp warning from the Universe. It underlines the message to accept change but when this card appears and resonates with you, it is a sign that you have refused to move on for too long, and now you're at risk of harming yourself or others around you. You wouldn't drink from stagnant water, and you shouldn't stay in a relationship that has gone sour either. Nor should you remain friends with someone or work somewhere that has grown toxic. Know when it's time for a change because it's just plain irresponsible otherwise.

The Death card reversed can speak to us less sharply, however. There are times when we're already going through changes—and these can be deep, personal, and life-altering—but we're not ready to share our new selves with the world. Death reversed is telling you that you're right to keep it to yourself. People around you might not be ready for the new you and you should use your intuition when judging the right time to share your transformation. When the time is right, the world will be ready.

Affirmation

I accept change. I accept my new self.

Temperance

♥

You've probably heard the phrase "work smarter, not harder" and if you've ever put that saying into practice, you'll know how true it is. The same applies to your relationships. You don't have to blunder blindly through life. You can figure out how to have a healthy and fulfilling life. Temperance is the way forward.

Common Portrayal

An angel stands with one foot in the stream and one on dry land, pouring water between two cups with perfect balance.

The Card Upright

Your heart rules your love life but you must balance it with what you know to be right, rather than what just feels right. A successful love life is about balance and Temperance tells us that the key to balance is keeping a calm and open mind. When you're trying to figure out how you feel about a relationship or person, let your thoughts and emotions alike come and go. Don't dwell on them. Like water flowing from a cup, let them spill out. Don't be ashamed or embarrassed by anything you think. Just let the thought be what it is. Then, when your thoughts and emotions are calm, consider the problem before you.

Don't just rely on your own intuition when dealing with matters of the heart. Seek all the advice and help you can get from your loved ones as well. Weight these perspectives. Be calm, even when you're feeling emotional—*especially* when you're feeling emotional. But also let your passions guide you. The key word there is *guide*. All your perspectives and thoughts and feelings are just guides to a better love life. In the end, you make the final call with a clear and balanced mind.

The Card Reversed

When reversed, Temperance is a reminder to look after ourselves. When our relationships and love life aren't going well, you may find yourself drinking too much, eating too much, and letting negative feelings dominate your mind. At times like that, Temperance reversed is a call for some self-healing by removing yourself from the source of your problems for a while and clearing your heart and mind.

Temperance reversed can also be a call to introspection. This is a private aspect of the card which you will probably recognize by how it resonates with you. You might be struggling with something internally and you aren't able to answer it. But you keep on picking at it like a sore tooth. When reversed, Temperance is suggesting you step back and take a fresh look at the situation, but from an internal perspective. You will find your answer when you realize the problem is caused by you trying to solve it.

Affirmation

I see myself from all sides. I know who I truly am.

The Devil

♥

We are all creatures of passion. It's what drives our love lives. It can take control of us, leading us to cross the line and never look back. Passion can also sometimes free us. Giving in to what you really want is pretty liberating. Once you make a deal with the Devil, though, there's no going back.

Common Portrayal

The Devil presides over his chained subjects. They are made in their master's image, horned and tailed.

The Card Upright

Like the flip side of the Temperance card, the Devil is all about giving into your urges—and facing the consequences. You can choose to stay in an unhealthy relationship if you want because it's exciting and sexy, so long as you know what the outcome will be. Staying loyal to a toxic friend from fear of losing them works exactly the same way. You'll know when the time has come to stop letting those desires and fears rule you. It's when this card speaks to you in a reading—usually in a way you can't ignore. The Devil isn't subtle.

Those same desires have power, however. Your passions can drive you to places you might not have imagined possible—if you can surf the wave, that is. A difficult partner might push you to excel in ways you couldn't on your own. You might also find great satisfaction in exploring new experiences in your love life. So long as you're safe and consenting, it's worthwhile indulging. You might surprise yourself.

The Card Reversed

When reversed, the Devil carries a similar message to the upright card, but with a twist. When upright, the card warns against being ruled by your desires. Reversed, it's telling you to confront where those desires are coming from. What is it that makes you choose the wrong partner over and over again? Why can't you stop treating people badly just because you feel bad? Questions like these come from a deep place and when the Devil reversed reaches out to you, it's probably time to answer a few of them.

You shouldn't attempt something like this alone. You will need the support of friends, family, and loved ones—and sometimes even professionals. But it's worth the time and effort because the Devil reversed also says that once you have answered these questions, you'll be free to move on to the next phase in your life. The urges and desires that caused you problems will vanish because you've addressed the problems at their source.

Affirmation

I walk my own path. I bow before no other.

The Tower

♥

We all know it's important to be at peace with change, but not all change is peaceful. Sometimes it can upend your world so completely that there's nothing left. Everything comes crashing down around you and you feel like your life is in ruins. That's because it is. The Tower stands—and falls—as a warning to be prepared.

Common Portrayal

Struck by a bolt of lightning, the Tower topples. People flee the ruin as the heavens fill with falling stars.

The Card Upright

People unfamiliar with the Tarot fear the Death or Devil cards. More experienced users know it's the Tower we need to watch out for—the change it promises will be significant and it's virtually impossible to deal with them once they're happening. When this card appears in your reading, it's alerting you to make sure you're at peace with your inner self, because your outer world can very easily come apart at the seams.

The Tower tells us that when deep, life-changing events overwhelm us, there's little we can do. But we can prepare ourselves in advance. What are your worst fears? What would turn your life upside down? A divorce? A death? The loss of a loved one? Don't wait until the Tower comes tumbling down—think about how you'd deal with those problems while you still have the chance. The card can't tell you what those problems will be, but you will know them when this card appears because it will speak to you so strongly. Pay attention to that warning and get your house in order, before it's too late.

The Card Reversed

When reversed, the Tower suggests an interesting opportunity for you. Ask yourself whether there's something big in your life that's holding you back. Something you have control over. Are you in a relationship that isn't good for you? Are your friends turning out to be not as reliable as you thought? Are you enabling a relative and suffering for it? The Tower reversed is telling you to break free from unhealthy relationships. Knock them to the ground and start over. You don't need that in your life.

This opportunity can be internal as well. Some of the problems we face are deep issues with deep foundations—long-held beliefs that are weighing you down, an overly critical self-image, or a lack of self-honesty, for example—but the Tower reversed is a reminder that you can bring it all down if you want to. Every last stone. Because you built those foundations yourself. Stands to reason that you're the one to wipe the slate clean.

Affirmation

I will make the most of whatever comes my way. I am ready for whatever happens.

The Star

♥

When it comes down to it, most of us are good people. Given the chance, we want to laugh or dance or love. We want to be happy. And when you're happy, you can't help but radiate that same energy. So how do you capture that energy in your daily life? The Star will illuminate the way.

Common Portrayal

A woman stands at the water's edge, one foot in the flow, the other on the bank, pouring water from jugs onto stream and shore alike. Above her, the skies are filled with stars.

The Card Upright

Finding your inner peace is a good idea at any time of life, but it's especially important in times of struggle or upheaval. When you're faced with questions about yourself and your relationships, you need to be the best version of yourself in order to answer those questions. You can't find a way forward with a clouded mind. As always, it starts with self-love and self-acceptance. Be honest with yourself and accept your flaws. You're only human. It's okay to try to do better and still fail, so long as you keep trying.

Instead of focusing on the negative, concentrate on pursuits that bring you joy and peace. They let your inner spark shine. You need to nurture that spark on a daily basis until it shines on its own. You'll see the effects on yourself and the world around you immediately. This is the Star's message—when you're busy with pursuits that bring you peace, you will spread your light into the world. Now ask yourself how living like that might affect your relationships or love life and you'll see the road ahead more clearly.

The Card Reversed

Reversed, the Star is like a beacon in the night, reminding you that light is everywhere. You just have to be looking in the right direction. This is a powerful card and demands patience and insight from you. Seeing the good in a bad situation is one of the hardest things to do. Your emotions interfere with your ability to make sense of everything, knocking you out of balance. The Star reversed urges you to make the effort to look deeply and think in the longer term. Is there a hidden silver lining here that you can draw strength from?

The Star reversed can also speak to you on an inner level, particularly when you're feeling disconnected from things in your love life that once brought you joy. Has the spark gone out of your relationship? Does your special someone not look at you the same way they used to? Are you struggling to remember why you fell for them in the first place? The Star reversed tells you to ask yourself why? What is the real cause that's sucking the light out of your relationship? As before, this card asks you to be honest with yourself and come to a balanced decision before moving on.

Affirmation

I will nurture the light within me. I will share it with the world.

The Moon

♥

Making the wrong call is an awful feeling (maybe only worse when done loudly and in public!). You just want the ground to open up and swallow you. How could you have been so wrong? The Moon is a fickle mistress. You must learn to be careful when navigating by her light.

Common Portrayal

The Moon rises between two towers at the water's edge. Below, a dog and a wolf howl at her while a crayfish crawls out of the water to gaze aloft.

The Card Upright

We like to think that we can make rational decisions, but it's actually really difficult. Our emotions and desires get the better of us and, to make it worse, we lie to ourselves about what we want. How on Earth can we have a happy love life or successful relationships when we're like this? When the Moon speaks to you in your reading, it's a sign that you need to pause for a moment and ask whether you're letting your feelings cloud your judgment.

When you feel this way, it's often because of a deeper issue that you're avoiding. You might not want to face up to a difficult situation and it's throwing you off balance. You can unpick this problem by going to the source. Follow your intuition—the main power of the Moon card—and ask what it is that's churning you up inside and messing with your judgment. Take the time to address it. You'll only continue getting things wrong if you don't.

The Card Reversed

When reversed, the Moon reinforces the importance of facing your inner issues, but it also raises the question of deception and illusion. Are you being completely honest with yourself about what you want from a relationship? Are you deliberately overlooking flaws in yourself or your partner? The Moon reversed is a call to put aside your fantasies and look at your situation under the cold light of day.

Deceit doesn't just come from within, either. Other people can lie to us just as easily. Are the people around you treating you with honesty and respect? Is someone hiding something from you? False friends who talk behind your back are no friends at all. Honesty is at the core of every relationship. Demand it from others as much as you demand it from yourself.

Affirmation

I see things as they truly are. Others see me as I truly am.

The Sun

When you're up, you're up and nothing's gonna get you down. You can ride that high for weeks sometimes and everyone around you can't help but be blown away by your amazing vibe. That's the Sun shining through you and there are few feelings better in life!

Common Portrayal

The Sun rises over a bountiful landscape. A child rides bareback on a white horse, carrying a fluttering banner.

The Card Upright

When the Sun appears in your reading, it's a message from the heavens to engage with your inner fire. Show the world what you're really made of. If you're looking for happiness in love or in your daily relationships, you won't find it by hiding away. Get out there, share your passions, and let the world see you as you really are—powerful, confident, and at home in your skin. Your energy will flood the people around you with inspiration and admiration.

What if you don't feel it though? The Sun card is a reassurance that you can start with baby steps. You have incredible strength inside you—not a bullish aggression, but the steady, eternal flame of the Sun itself. Bit by bit, when you feel up to it, start with sharing just a little of yourself with someone. A secret. A dream. A desire. Take it a day at a time. Before you know it, your Sun will be ready to rise for all to see.

The Card Reversed

The Sun reversed can be a reminder to lighten up. When your love life is going according to plan, it's easy to become discouraged. One way to combat this is to let your inner child come out to play. Find an activity that's nothing more than pure fun and make time for it. Share it with your special someone if you can—when they see you in your happy place, it can reinvigorate their feelings for you. When you nurture your inner joy, it makes you more attractive to everyone around you and helps you see your relationships with a more positive perspective. The Sun reversed is a call to make sure your inner child is getting the quality time they need.

Sometimes, however, the Sun reversed is a warning. You'll know when this happens because you'll feel like the card is speaking to you directly. Have you been lording it over your special someone, taking advantage of their devotion to you? Have you been taking them for granted and just presuming that they'll still keep running along at your heels? A little humility might be in order—the Sun reversed is a quiet nudge from the Universe to check your ego. Be gentler with those you love.

Affirmation

I will seek joy. I will not hide it.

Judgment

♥

Everyone talks about their fifteen minutes of fame, but the truth is that we're small players in a vast game. Every now and then, though, the spotlight falls on us and we're called to step up and make a difference. Will you answer the call? Judgment awaits.

Common Portrayal

An angel appears in the heavens and sounds a call on his celestial trumpet. Down below, people rise from the Earth to meet the angel's song.

The Card Upright

When Judgment appears in your reading, it's a call to prepare for major change. You may have seen change appear as a theme in other Tarot cards, but here it has the potential to be life-changing—and what's more, it's change driven entirely by you. The Judgment card tells you that when you're confronted with big decisions about your life, your relationships, or your special someone, you need to make sure you're in the driving seat. It's a demand for conscious action on your part. It's time to step up.

You must approach these big decisions with balance, melding intuition and logic. Ask for guidance. Pray, if such is your inclination. Meditate. Get in touch with the best version of yourself and ask for their advice. Seek the help of friends and family. You will know when great change is upon you. Let go of your frustrations and fears and desires and be guided by your highest ideals, your most loving motivations. You're at the end of a journey. Finish it in style.

The Card Reversed

Judgment reversed is the calm before the storm. Great changes in your love life are on the horizon but you may not be ready. When this card speaks to you in its reversed position, ask yourself whether there are still issues you need to address before moving on to the next phase of your relationship. Has your special someone suggested taking

81

things to the next level? How does that make you feel? If you're not ready, you must make this clear. Do you feel like you want something from your partner, but they don't seem ready to give it? Do the two of you need to make some changes first?

When reversed, Judgment can also be a call to give a voice to your inner critic. Have you been closing your eyes to problems in your love life? Perhaps your conscience is prodding you and you'd rather it didn't. There's a reason for that. Stop and listen to that inner voice. What is it telling you? What can you be doing to be a better partner? Who can you be treating better in your relationships? Answer these questions. They will hold you back if you don't.

Affirmation

I know my place. Nothing will keep me from it.

The World

♥

You've come a long way to get where you are, and you should take the time to enjoy your accomplishments. Every ending is a new beginning but when you start over, you'll do so with the benefit of everything you've learned. The World is yours!

Common Portrayal

A woman dances in a laurel wreath, robed and bearing symbols of power. Mythical beasts surround her, symbolizing her harmony with the Universe.

The Card Upright

When the World appears in your reading, take a moment to rejoice. This card is the summation of the Major Arcana and represents the best version of yourself. It's telling you to remember who you are and what you've been through. You can draw strength and inspiration from your experiences and relationships, even the horrible ones. You may have made mistakes along the way, but if you've been honest with yourself, then they're just honest mistakes. We all make them. What matters is where you are now and where you can go from here. Which is anywhere.

Even with such a positive card, you might not quite feel like you're on top of the World. Don't worry—a card as powerful as this one is a guide to finding your way to where you need to be. And that way is actually the way you have come. Look back at your recent experiences and your recent relationships (and not just the horrible ones!) and see what they can teach you about yourself. Take real-time to be open and honest with yourself about this. Then consider the card again. If your recent experiences are a journey, where has it led you? If you could go anywhere from here, where would you go?

The Card Reversed

When reversed, the World is a message that you have unfinished business. You can't complete your journey until you tend to outstanding matters. These might be personal—a relationship needing closure, a loved one needing a farewell—or they might relate to your career or family. You'll know what these issues are because they'll have been bothering you for weeks and now, you'll be feeling all uncomfortable about them while you're reading this. That's good. That's the Universe telling you to deal with them. You'd be wise to listen.

In a similar vein, the World reversed can be a warning that you've drifted off-course right before getting where you wanted to be. Maybe you've let your love life run stale or neglected a friendship and now it feels like it's too late. The World reversed is telling you that it's never too late. Reassess what you want and need from yourself and the people around you and restate it clearly. Here, at the end of the road, it matters more than ever that you finish your journey properly.

Affirmation

I am ready to complete my journey. At last, I am who I have always wanted to be.

Chapter 4: The Minor Arcana

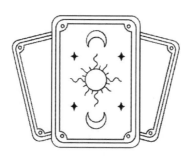

Suit of Wands

Ace of Wands

♥

Beginnings are wonderful times, so full of potential. That honeymoon period at the start of a relationship. Getting to know new friends. Don't waste the opportunities these times bring. The Ace of Wands will point out the way to making the most of them.

Common Portrayal

A hand emerges from a cloud, holding a single wand that sprouts green shoots. In the distance, a castle stands alone.

The Card Upright

The Ace of Wands is all about possibilities. It asks you to look at your current situation. Does it have the potential to become something fulfilling? Does it speak to your passions? Are you ready to embark on something new like a friendship, relationship, or other romantic entanglements? When the Ace of Wands appears in your reading, it's a suggestion to lead with your creative energies. Go ahead and start something new and exciting.

On an internal level, the Ace of Wands is a reminder to always think about how you can improve yourself as a person. People who are successful in love are also people who give some thought to their own growth. Is there a way you can better yourself? A new hobby, course of study, or approach to living? A new you, energized and creative, will be far more attractive to the people around you.

The Card Reversed

Reversed, the Ace of Wands cautions you to make sure you're ready to embark on a path laid before you. Do you have second thoughts about starting a new relationship? Are warning bells ringing in your head? You should listen to them, take a moment, and assess whether this is what you really want. When starting out on a new path in life, you need to be sure.

If you're struggling to figure out whether a new person or situation is right for you, it's worth asking yourself why. What's stopping you from making a decision one way or the other? Why aren't you fired up about this new opportunity? Is it really speaking to your passions, your inner fire? The Ace of Wands reversed is telling you to be discerning. Only walk the road that will take you where you need to go.

Affirmation

I engage my passions. All will see my inner flame.

Two of Wands

♥

Patience and planning are what it's all about. You know where you want to go in life so now it's time to get creative and figure out how you're going to get there. Don't just charge blindly ahead. The Two of Wands is your reminder to take the time to plan it out.

Common Portrayal

Standing on his castle battlements, a man holds a wand in one hand and a globe in the other. A second wand stands to his side as he surveys the world beyond his home.

The Card Upright

When you know what you want in life it's tempting to just go for it. Sometimes, however, you need to keep your urges in check. You control your passions, not the other way around. Plan your moves carefully, making sure they're always in tune with your own inner drives and energy. What makes your special someone tick? What does your pushy relative really want? How can you best impress the boss? If you plan your approach, you'll find answers to the questions before you.

The Two of Wands can also speak to you during your reading if there are decisions you still need to make. Are you putting something off because you don't have all your ducks in a row? Is an exciting opportunity waiting for you, but you're feeling nervous about taking it? The Two of Wands is telling you that you're right to think things through—but that you shouldn't delay for too long. Get out there and see what the world has in store for you!

The Card Reversed

The Two of Wands reversed is a signal to reassess your goals. When this card speaks to you during a reading, ask yourself if you're headed in the right direction. Is your relationship progressing as you want it to? Are your friendships and career fulfilling? If not, you should take some time to figure out why? Are you clear with yourself about what you really want? If not, how can you be honest with others?

When reversed, the Two of Wands can also be a reminder to make sure that your latest passionate idea is founded in reality. The Wands suit is all about your inner drives, after all, so it makes sense for this card to call attention to that. Similar to the upright version of the card, this requires some planning, but the reversed Two of Wands is asking you to check whether your idea is even possible. Have you let fantasy run away with you? Is a dose of cold reality in order?

Affirmation

I see the way forward. I made it myself.

Three of Wands

♥

Taking control of your life is as rewarding as anything else, but it comes with a heap of responsibilities. The most important of those is to keep control of your life and use it to grow as a person. The Three of Wands is your guide along the way.

Common Portrayal

A robed traveler gazes at the vast open spaces awaiting them. Three wands stand at their side; the traveler grasps one.

The Card Upright

The Three of Wands is all about personal responsibility and personal growth combined. You should be in charge of what happens in your love life and your relationships but sometimes you also need to push yourself beyond your comfort zone. Ask yourself in what ways you could challenge yourself or your assumptions. Do you dare break your own limits? The Three of Wands is telling you to try because you'll open up whole new avenues of adventure if you do.

The card can also be a reminder to take account of any obstacles that may be waiting for you. Does your special someone have a jealous ex? Will your new career or hobby cause problems at home? Are you about to put a friendship under pressure? The Three of Wands isn't a warning to avoid these obstacles—instead, it's telling you to prepare for them. If you're being true to yourself, then it's okay to face hurdles from time to time. Take the time in advance to figure out how to deal with them—don't wait until the problem is looming over you!

The Card Reversed

When reversed, the Three of Wands is all about reassurance—often when you haven't followed the advice of the upright card! If you're facing challenges and obstacles that lie outside your comfort zone and can't figure out why life is so hard, ask yourself if you really took the time to be ready for where you're going. Do you need to step back and plan a better way forward?

When you're overwhelmed by frustration and failure, the Three of Wands reversed is a reminder that we can learn from our defeats as much as from our victories. You did everything you were supposed to, tried your best to figure out the best approach, and still you failed. That's not because there's anything wrong with you. That's just life. Pick yourself up, dust yourself off, and get back out there, wiser, smarter, and more ready for what's to come.

Affirmation

I will set my own limits. Then I will break them.

Four of Wands

♥

Home is where the heart is so it's important to keep a connection with those closest to you. Even when you're out in the wilds of life, take the time to touch base every now and then. Keeping your feet on the ground is always a good idea and the Four of Wands will show you how.

Common Portrayal

Framed by four wands, a couple dance together beneath flowering garlands. Behind them, a family gathers at the gates to a great castle.

The Card Upright

It's not where you're at that matters. It's where you're coming from. That's the message of the Four of Wands. Yes, you should explore all that life and love have to offer you, but don't forget your roots. Few of us make it through life single-handedly, so think about the people who helped you along your road. Have you neglected your relationships with them? You did not get where you are today without the love and support of people around you. Friends. Lovers. Family. Exes. Reach out to them. Rebuild bonds that might have eroded over time.

The Four of Wands is also a reminder to take a breather. Have you been on a wild dating binge? Partying until dawn with your friends? Is it worth putting all that to one side for a while to center yourself and refuel? You can't sustain meaningful relationships if you're completely burned out. Take the time to assess how you've been treating people—some journeys only make sense when you look back at them.

The Card Reversed

The Four of Wands reversed can be a warning to check in on those closest to you. For a card so focused on your connections to the most important people in your life, it's no surprise that when reversed, it's a reminder to consider the needs of these people. If the card is speaking to you, it may be a sign that you've been overly focused on your own journey. Spend some time and energy helping others along their own road before returning to your own. Your path will be richer for it.

There's an interesting inner aspect to the Four of Wands reversed as well. The upright card talks about honoring the milestones you have reached along the way—when reversed, the card suggests that you should honor those achievements in private... for now. Crowing about your gains may make you feel great, but it can cause others to feel resentful or jealous. You should always be proud of what you have accomplished in life, but you also need to balance that against the feelings of your loved ones. Sensitivity is the way forward here.

Affirmation

I return to my center. My loved ones welcome me home.

Five of Wands

♥

People don't always agree with each other, and those disagreements can become pretty heated. Marriages end, as do friendships. Relationships fall apart. Careers derail. But does conflict always have to be a bad thing? The Five of Wands shows how to deal with and learn from your battles.

Common Portrayal

Five figures clad in clashing colors brandish wands. They look as if they have just begun a fight—or just ended one.

The Card Upright

The Five of Wands is all about conflict and the changes it brings. If you find yourself out of sorts with the important people in your life, this card is telling you to stop and listen. You don't have to put your own ideas aside, but you do need to pay close attention to what others are saying. Is there a way you can see things from their perspective that will help you reach an agreement? Does their behavior make more sense if you try to understand the reasons behind it? All good communication starts with listening, and good communication is the key to defusing conflict.

The Five of Wands also suggests that conflict might not be bad. A productive brainstorming session at work will certainly see you butting heads with people, but that's a good thing if it produces strong results. It's the same in your personal life—sometimes you need to thrash out your issues with your loved ones. Tempers flare, but if you can keep your urges in check, you can put that energy to good use together. Just keep communicating.

The Card Reversed

The Five of Wands reversed focuses your attention on your inner world and tells you to embrace conflict. Or, rather, to use it to your advantage. The opinions of those close to you can be a source of conflicting ideas but you can use this as a way to analyze your own opinions. When someone's words get under our skin, there's usually a reason for that.

Ask yourself why and see if you can draw some insight from their perspective.

If you struggle with confrontation, the Five of Wands reversed can serve as a reassurance that it's okay to clash with people sometimes. It can be very uncomfortable but if you keep your head and fight the urge to lose your temper, it's possible to make your thoughts heard, even when the other person doesn't want to listen. Let them flounder about and lose their cool. State your truths strongly and clearly. Be firm and don't back down until you make your feelings known. Strong and calm is the way forward here.

Affirmation

I do not fear conflict. It shows me who I am.

Six of Wands

♥

Sing when you're winning! You shouldn't be bashful about your accomplishments—life is tough enough as it is without being your own worst critic. Be proud of who you are and what you've done and if that sounds easier said than done, then let the Six of Wands give you a shove in the right direction.

Common Portrayal

Crowned with a garland and holding another atop a wand, a rider enjoys the adulation of the crowd.

The Card Upright

The Six of Wands is your invitation to celebrate where you are in life. And if it doesn't seem like there's much to celebrate, this card is a suggestion to change your perspective, look more closely at what you have, and perhaps appreciate it a little more. Small victories are victories all the same, and each step we take builds on the one before. It's the same in your relationships, so don't be discouraged—you build a strong foundation one brick at a time.

When you do feel on top of things, the Six of Wands encourages you to make the most of the moment. Enjoy the praises of your loved ones. Let everyone see how happy you are with how your life is going. Don't crow—no one appreciates that—but humbly accept and show joy in the good things that life brings you. These moments are fuel for leaner times, so nurture them!

The Card Reversed

Reversed, the Six of Wands has advice on dealing with success and the praise of others. The upright card tells you to take pride when life is going well without trampling on the feelings of others, and the reversed card reinforces this. You will damage your relationships and yourself by letting an over-inflated ego trumpet in everyone's face. Learn when to dial it back. Learn how to read the room. Find that balance and your loved ones will want nothing more than to share in your joy.

The Six of Wands reversed also tells you to set your own measures of success. Receiving praise from people you care about feels great, but you want to be praised for things that matter to you, not to them. You want them to be happy for you on your terms. Don't change your goals just to please others. Set your own standards and live by them. Do this clearly and humbly, and people will respect you.

Affirmation

My joy is a banquet. All are welcome.

Seven of Wands

♥

When jealousy rears its green and snarly head, be on your guard. You may have achieved great things, but chances are someone is less than pleased with you and probably more than a little envious. Don't worry about it—the Seven of Wands will help you keep them at bay!

Common Portrayal

A figure stands atop a mountain, warding off half a dozen wands with one single wand. The figure's shoes are mismatched.

The Card Upright

There's no avoiding it sometimes—you hook up with that special someone, score a great promotion, join an exciting new group of friends and you couldn't be happier. Except there's always *that* person who has to rain on your parade. So, what do you do? The Seven of Wands is clear in this—you stand your ground. If you got where you are fair and square, don't you dare give up just because someone is jealous!

The way to cope with this kind of situation is to think ahead. As your life starts to fall into shape, spend a little time thinking about people who might be upset by this and figuring out what to say in advance. Don't wait until they're in your face. Plan out ahead of time how you'd respond, what you'd say, how far you'd let it go before shutting them down. Then, should anyone come along to ruin your good vibes, it won't knock you off-course. You'll already know how to react.

The Card Reversed

The Seven of Wands reversed can be a warning, however, not to assume ill intentions on the part of others. Do you feel like people are always criticizing you or are never happy for you? Ask yourself if you're thinking clearly. Are people really *always* down on you? Honestly, they have better things to be worrying about than you. Instead, ask yourself why you might feel like you're disappointing your loved ones. Do you have an unresolved issue that's causing you to see everything they do in a bad light? If so, that's something worth addressing.

Reversed, the Seven of Wands can also offer guidance when you're feeling overwhelmed. Have you taken on too much? Do you feel like you've agreed to too many appointments or have made promises you can't keep? In that case, you need to rein in your enthusiasm and think about what is realistic to accomplish. Being a driven person is great, but you need to set a pace in life and love that works for you and those around you.

Affirmation

I stand firm. Nothing deters my good intentions.

Eight of Wands

♥

Being in tune with life and in tune with your own drives gives you an energy that can't be stopped. So, don't try. Let the universe carry you forward—it's bigger and stronger than you anyway—and let the Eight of Wands guide you to new adventures!

Common Portrayal

Eight wands hurtle through a clear blue sky. Below, a river winds peacefully on its way.

The Card Upright

The Eight of Wands is a highly energetic card, filled with positive energy. That's the energy you need to harness to make the most of life's opportunities, and the best way to do that is to align your inner drives with what's going on around you. Successful relationships and a happy love life are much easier to achieve when the things you want are in tune with the other people in your life. When you're in sync, you can just go with the flow and enjoy the ride. But you have to seize the moment.

So, don't wait around. Practice listening to your loved ones and figure out how you can make your drives match up with what they want. In your career, try to get a sense of which direction your work environment is moving, then align your own moves with that. This doesn't mean that you should do things you don't agree with. But you exist in the world, so you need to make sure that what you want can work. The results will be startling—you'll feel like life is just taking care of itself.

The Card Reversed

When reversed, the Eight of Wands can be a reminder to make sure you aren't rushing ahead without considering what lies ahead. You may feel filled with energy and determination and, once you take the plunge, there's no turning back. So, be certain that you're ready and have thought through what the road ahead looks like. This applies to new relationships, career changes, and even new phases in existing relationships. Use the energy you're feeling but do so with a clear head.

Interestingly, the Eight of Wands reversed can also be a warning to stop putting things off. Do you feel the urge to move forward in a relationship but can't bring yourself to take that first step? At times like that, the card is a nudge to get moving, and for the same reasons—you need to be in tune with the world and act accordingly. Hanging back when you should be moving forward is just as bad as rushing ahead when you should be careful. As always, it's about balance. You, your drives, and the world around you, are all synced up.

Affirmation

I am in tune with the world. I go with the flow.

Nine of Wands

♥

From time to time, life slaps you in the face. Hard. And then it laughs. It's horrible—no point in pretending otherwise—but there's often nothing you can do about it. You have to pick yourself up and get back in the game, even when it's the last thing you want to do. Don't be discouraged, though—the Nine of Wands will help you through.

Common Portrayal

A wounded figure leans on a wand, looking darkly at eight more that cluster close at hand.

The Card Upright

You're going to suffer. People lie, let you down, cheat on you—or you lie and cheat on them! We're imperfect. But when adversity comes your way, is it really the time to curl up into a ball and wait for it all to go away? There are times to stand tall, and the Nine of Wands is asking you to lift your head and refuse to back down. If you have been true to yourself and honest with yourself and your loved ones, then you'll be like a rock in the storm. Let people around you rage and bluster. Stay firm.

If you're finding it hard to hold your ground, the Nine of Wands is also a reminder that you don't have to do so alone. If you're living your life in harmony with the world around you, there will be people ready to fight your corner. Call on them. You may be a rock in the storm, but you're not an island. Your loved ones want to help you. Let them.

The Card Reversed

When the Nine of Wands reversed speaks to you during your reading, ask yourself whether you're feeling over-whelmed by your situation. Are you struggling to make sense of your relationships and the people you care about? If so, this card is a call to pause and assess where the problem is coming from. Be clear, calm, and honest with yourself. Give yourself the time to balance your desires, then re-engage when your energy levels are up to the task. Take what space you need, but don't hide in there.

Sometimes, however, your own weariness and confusion can cloud your perceptions. If you're struggling in life and relationships, you won't have a clear outlook. Your reactions will be colored by your emotions, and you'll see negativity where there may not be any. Are your loved ones really down on you? Or are you just too worn out to tell the difference? If so, you know you need to focus on your own self-care, so you're ready to meet the world on even ground.

Affirmation

I stand my ground. I am not alone.

Ten of Wands

♥

Being happy is hard work and you won't find the happiness you want without that work. It's worth it, though. The sense of accomplishment that comes from building a life you love is such a special feeling and one you should pursue. The Ten of Wands is your guide to accomplishing that.

Common Portrayal

Carrying a burden of ten wands, a figure labors towards a nearby town. Soon, their journey will be over.

The Card Upright

The Ten of Wands is all about doing the work needed to achieve your goals and accepting the responsibilities that come with fulfillment. Even if your goal seems a long way off, with obstacles aplenty, this card is telling you to persevere. As always, the way forward is with a clear head, an honest heart, and taking one step at a time. Just like the bundle of wands on the card, many problems seem like a single overwhelming mass, but you can break them down into more manageable issues.

The card is also a reminder that getting what you want in life or love doesn't mean you abandon all the things you learned along the way. Stay humble. Continue to treat your loved ones with compassion. Be like the traveler who has come home from a long journey—be happy where you are but bring that happiness into the lives of people around you. It's a responsibility. When you have achieved something important to you, pay it forward and spread the love to someone else in turn.

The Card Reversed

The Ten of Wands reversed asks you to examine the burdens you're carrying. Have you taken on too much? Are you trying to be there for too many people (or one or two very demanding individuals) and not spending enough energy on dealing with your own problems? It's good to help your loved ones but it is not your job to carry all the woes of the world. You can't help anyone if your own life falls apart around you.

Similarly, you can ask for help. It's an obvious point but we can get so caught up in our own problems that we forget to look up from time to time and ask others for a hand. You can and should share your hopes and fears with those closest to you. It's unhealthy to bottle everything up inside. Learn to reach out and ask for support when you need it. The people who care about you will want to help.

Affirmation

I take the final step. At last, I am home.

Page of Wands

♥

You don't always have to know where you're going. Having an open mind and a willingness to jump into something new makes for an exciting life. Sure, there are risks but they can be worth it. The Page of Wands is here to give you a nudge out the door.

Common Portrayal

In a barren landscape, a fancifully clad Page examines a wand. Green shoots bud from its length.

The Card Upright

The Page of Wands is all about new ideas, particularly if those ideas will take you somewhere completely unexpected like a new relationship or a different social circle. Be open to new experiences and seeing new people. Is there someone you had never considered dating before, for example? Are they catching your attention somehow? Step out of your comfort zone and take a chance on them. There are times to be calm and sensible and there are times to leap into the unknown and see where it takes you. Are you ready?

If you aren't, the card has some interesting advice in that regard. Just like a page serves a knight or other lord or lady, you can seek the advice of someone more experienced or knowledgeable than yourself. Is there someone in your life you look to as a wise mentor? Do you know someone who has experienced love and loss and all that comes with it? Can they share their relationship insights with you? What would they say about being open to seeing new people and taking exciting chances in your love life? Don't be afraid to ask!

The Card Reversed

Reversed, the Page of Wands is a reassurance when life isn't quite turning out how you expected. If you're trying to explore new ideas and experiences or meet new people and you're finding it a struggle, the Page of Wands reversed suggests that maybe the time isn't right yet. Don't force things. Let friendships blossom naturally. If your special someone isn't responding to you in the way you hoped, ease off a little. They may not be ready for what you have in mind just yet.

Alternatively, try to look at your situation from a new perspective. You might still be able to move in the direction you want if you come at it from a different angle. Are you struggling to make yourself understood by someone? Is there another way to get your point across? The Page of Wands reversed is a reminder that there are many ways to reach a goal. Try a few.

Affirmation

I am open to new experiences. This is how I grow.

Knight of Wands

Saddle up and hit the road because your hour has come. You know what you want and it's time to go and get it. You're armed and armored and anyone who stands in your way will regret it. It's time to ride out with the Knight of Wands!

Common Portrayal

Mounted atop a trusty steed, the Knight of Wands holds a single wand aloft. His horse rears against the barren landscape.

The Card Upright

The Knight of Wands leads by example and so should you. Be bold. Be courageous. Take calculated risks and reach for the stars. Don't be put off by obstacles—treat them as opportunities to show everyone what you're made of. Like a knight slaying dragons, go toe-to-toe with whatever stands in your way. Embody the knightly virtues of compassion, honor, and courage, but don't shy away from confrontation. You're more than ready for this.

So long as you keep a clear head about this and don't trample on the people around you as you forge a path for yourself, you'll find yourself becoming more attractive. Success and determination put a shine on you, so make the most of that. Let that special someone see you powering ahead in life. They might just decide that they want some of that shine in their own life, and where better to find it than with you?

The Card Reversed

The Knight of Wands reversed is a warning to avoid acting impulsively or inconsiderately. When your drives and desires are all aflame, it's tempting to rush ahead without a thought in the world. Trouble is, you may well trample a few innocents beneath your hooves along the way. Take care that your passions aren't blinding you to the needs of those around you.

The card can also speak to your frustrations. Are you raring to do but life keeps getting in the way? Are you keen to embark on a new relationship but there are all these hurdles in your way? At times like this, the Knight of Wands reversed is a reminder to consider a different approach. Can you come at your problems from another angle? What if you work smart instead of just working hard? There's more than one way to get what you want.

Affirmation

Every challenge helps me grow. Every victory makes me more compassionate.

Queen of Wands

♥

You're a social butterfly, flitting from one wonderful encounter to another, spreading joy with every beat of your wings. Your passions are engaged, you're living the life you want, and you're at peace with yourself. And if you aren't, the Queen of Wands would like a few words with you.

Common Portrayal

Enthroned and robed, the Queen holds a wand in one hand and a sunflower in the other. A black cat sits at her feet.

The Card Upright

The Queen of Wands is a call to put yourself out there. You have so much to offer, so make sure people can see that. Be optimistic and determined about what you want but keep an eye on your loved ones—they will benefit from your presence when you're full of life. Share your joy. Don't be afraid to use your energy and passion to inspire others. Show them what a life well-lived looks like.

The black cat on the card speaks to another aspect of the Queen of Wands, and that's your shadow self. Your dark side. Your hidden passions and secret desires. Don't hide these inside—they need to breathe and live. Take the time to indulge in your private pleasures and nurture your shadow so it can live in harmony with your public face. When all the aspects of your personality are in balance, you will thrive.

The Card Reversed

When reversed, the Queen of Wands is telling that it's actually okay if you don't much feel like being a social butterfly and spreading joy as you dance through the fields of your love. Maybe you would rather be an antisocial recluse and roll around in the fields of your unmade bed while watching TV and eating things you shouldn't. Great. Go for it. You deserve it. You need to take the time to nourish yourself. Don't let people judge you. You do you. You're a queen, after all.

Part of this can be because you've let others push you around or run your life for too long. We do need others to step in and help from time to time, but there's a limit to that kind of interference and you need to know where yours lies—and when to tell people to step off and give you the space you need. You're not here to meet the expectations of other people. Set your own goals. When you're ready to pursue them, you'll know.

Affirmation

I know who I am. I spread joy.

King of Wands

♥

Some people don't have a clue until someone else shows them the way. Some follow and some lead, helping others achieve great things through their strength of vision. If you find yourself in either position, seek an audience with the King of Wands—his advice is indispensable.

Common Portrayal

The King sits on his throne, a wand resting in one hand. At his side, a small lizard rests.

The Card Upright

The King of Wands is about being a leader and using that to achieve your goals. But it's not a short-term thing. This is a powerful card and so demands something from you. It's asking you to live your whole life with intent and vision. It's telling you to learn what you want and shape your whole life towards achieving it, be that a life partner, a career move, a new set of friends, a reinvigorated relationship, or whatever. With this clear and determined approach, you will inspire those around you and carry them with you.

There's a level of maturity required here, a degree of balance. But if you can achieve that, you'll find people looking up to you and coming to you for advice. Now is the time to share your passions and drives with them and inspire them to join you in support. You will, over time, build a loyal group of friends and loved ones, all driven by your leadership. Together, you can accomplish anything.

The Card Reversed

Reversed, the King of Wands asks you whether you're ready to step into the role of leader. Do you have what it takes to inspire people around you? Do you instead need to work on your communication skills or find better ways to listen to what your loved ones are telling you? Do you maybe think that you're the only one who can figure your problems out? The King of Wands reversed is a reminder that you aren't alone and that you need to pay closer attention to those you care about.

The card reversed can also be a warning not to set unrealistic goals for yourself. The best way to find happiness in life is to understand your limitations. You may not be ready for that big career move, or you may not be socially comfortable enough to start dating again. The King of Wands reversed tells you to take the time to check. Ask yourself if you're running before you can walk. What more work do you need to do?

Affirmation

I am not alone. Many follow where I lead.

Suit of Cups

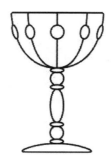

Ace of Cups

♥

Being open in life and love is at once refreshing and exhilarating. Good experiences come your way and you reflect them right back at the world. Your heart is full to bursting and you've still more to give. That's the ideal, anyway, and the Ace of Cups will help you achieve it.

Common Portrayal

A hand emerges from a cloud bearing a cup that overflows with streams of water. A dove descends above the cup as its waters mingle with the ocean below.

The Card Upright

The Ace of Cups is about having an open heart. That's really all there is to it. Like all Ace cards, it talks about beginnings but is laser-focused on matters of the heart. The card tells you that you can find real love and fulfillment, but you cannot do so with a closed heart. You need to be open to new possibilities, dare to risk a new relationship, and take a chance on someone you hadn't considered. Always, self-love comes first, and with it self-respect. With those as your guide, be open to what comes your way

Love flows both ways, of course, and the Ace of Cups is also a reminder to be giving. Are there ways you can help others? Make compassion your guide—where does it lead you? Most importantly, do not be cynical or harsh about love, even if you're not feeling it in your life at the moment. *Especially* if you're not feeling it. The Ace of Cups tells you that it's your responsibility to spread love and compassion. The more you do, the more it will come back to you.

The Card Reversed

The upright Ace of Cups mentions touches on self-love but when reversed, it's front and center. It's not shy about it either—the card all but demands you fill yourself up with love. Focus on what brings you joy and pursue it. It can be personal and private or public and out there for everyone to see but the key is that it matters to you, that it nourishes you and brings you to a place of peace and happiness deep inside.

The Ace of Cups reversed can also be a nudge to be more open with your emotions. Do you struggle to express yourself? Do you keep your cards close to your chest? You might have good reason to do so but be careful not to bottle your feelings up. Find ways to express yourself to give your feelings air. You can do this in private, of course—there's real freedom in letting it all out without any boundaries or judgment. So long as the end goal is love for yourself and nurturing your needs, you can just let it rip.

Affirmation

I am open to love. Most of all, I am open to love from myself.

Two of Cups

♥

Being on the same wavelength as your special someone can take your love life to a whole new level. The synchronization it brings is more than the sum of its parts—you quite literally are building something bigger than either of you. The Two of Cups has some advice on how to find that kind of togetherness in your own life.

Common Portrayal

A couple joins hands to hold a pair of cups. Above them floats a *caduceus*—a mystical symbol with two snakes entwined—and a winged lion head.

The Card Upright

The Two of Cups symbolizes the importance of letting others into your life. It's an encouragement to grow through sharing. It's easy to see this card as being about falling in love or a new relationship, and there's truth in that. If your heart is pointing you in a certain direction, sure, go ahead and see what life has in store. But it's not just about your love life.

For such an unassuming card, the Two of Cups carries a very deep message. It's telling you plain and simple that you can't move forward in life if you don't have a heart that is open and loving. It's telling you to communicate with the people around you, listen as much as share, and accept their viewpoints, to show compassion. It's easy to love people who are like us—the real power is in being able to love those who are very different.

The Card Reversed

The Two of Cups reversed focuses on self-love, much like the Ace of Cups. Where the Two of Cups differs is that it's prompting you to consider self-love as a way to improve your relationships with others, rather than just as a purely personal goal. When your cup is overflowing with love, you can't help but spread that around. The Two of Cups reversed is your reminder to embody that wherever you can.

When reversed, the Two of Cups can also highlight failures of communication. Have you fallen out with someone in your life like a friend or family member? Are you and your partner fighting more than seems reasonable? This card is asking you to check whether you're communicating clearly, openly, and honestly. Take the time and space to share your thoughts and concerns, then listen with just as much openness and honesty to what the other person is saying. Can you find common ground somewhere?

Affirmation

Love flows from me. Love flows to me.

Three of Cups

♥

Your closest friends are your fiercest allies. Some of us are fortunate to have families that are just as supportive, but not everyone is that lucky. But the family you make for yourself from those you love and trust is one that will never desert you. The Three of Cups will help you find that family.

Common Portrayal

Three women dance in a circle, each holding a cup in the air. Flowers, fruit, and a pumpkin lie at their feet.

The Card Upright

The Three of Cups is a reminder not to face life alone. Build a circle of close and trusted friends around, a family you have found and forged yourselves, and draw on them in times of need—and be there for them when they need you! As with all Cups cards, the road to close friendships of this sort is love. Love yourself and those around you and you'll find it builds the strongest of walls, the brightest of homes.

The card also suggests that you build on those foundations by embarking on a shared project of some kind with your found family. This can be a business venture, a vacation, a retreat, or a weekend hiking—it doesn't actually matter. What's important is that you and your closest friends are sharing activities and time together, building and strengthening bonds. The experiences this gives us can often provide answers to questions we're struggling with.

The Card Reversed

Reversed, the Three of Cups carries a couple of interesting suggestions that stem from the same place. As a card of friendship and cooperation, when reversed, the card is telling you that it's okay to take time away from your friends and social life. Maybe you need to recharge, think things through, or just get away from the world for a while. If you're struggling, ask yourself whether a little me-time is in order.

The Three of Cups reversed can also be a warning about becoming involved with others when you probably shouldn't. Being attracted to someone who is already in another relationship. Sharing secrets with someone who isn't meant to hear them. Interfering when it's none of your business. These are all examples of times when it would be better to keep your distance. When this card speaks to you during your reading, ask yourself if there are areas of your life where you could dial it down a little and give people more space.

Affirmation

We are one. We are invincible.

Four of Cups

♥

We can't all be social butterflies 24-7. Nor do we need to be endless wells of support, always giving, never taking a moment for ourselves. Do you want burnout? Because that's how you get burnout. Drink from the Four of Cups and learn the importance of just letting the world do its thing for a while.

Common Portrayal

A figure sits in thought under a tree. Cups sit on the ground or are offered from a cloud.

The Card Upright

The Four of Cups is a complex card that talks about isolation—specifically isolation you choose yourself. There are plenty of reasons to take a step back from the world and when this card appears in your reading, ask yourself if now is one of them. Do you need a breather in your relationship? Is this relationship right for you? Listen to how your heart answers those kinds of questions. At times like this, it can speak more clearly than your head.

This card can also be a call to look inwards and ask whether you've committed yourself to something you don't really believe in. A friendship. Even a relationship. If this card is speaking to you, is it because you haven't quite settled where you'd hoped? It's important to take time for introspection and make sure you're listening to your heart. As always, you must balance what your heart wants with what is rational and practical—don't neglect one over the other.

The Card Reversed

The Four of Cups reversed speaks to a sense of disillusionment—a feeling that things just haven't worked out the way you'd hoped. The upright version of the card touches on this, but when reversed, the card is asking you to take a long look at where you are in love and life. If you're feeling like things haven't worked out, ask yourself why? What were you hoping for? Why hasn't it happened? Can you change things? Should you?

That last point is an important one. While life might not work out the way you want, it can work out the way you need. Do you just need to accept an uncomfortable result, knowing it will be better in the long run? That's a hard pill to swallow. Take a while to imagine the better future that a sacrifice now will bring. It can be worth taking the medicine now to avoid problems further down the line.

Affirmation

I listen to my heart. I hear nothing else.

Five of Cups

♥

Heartbreak is brutal. For something that's supposed to be an emotion, you feel it like a punch in the gut, like it's physical. We all face it and it's just as crushing each time. But we can survive heartbreak, even grow from it. The Five of Cups are brimming with insight into how.

Common Portrayal

A figure stares down at three fallen cups, while two stand upright behind him. Across a river lies a castle.

The Card Upright

There is no easy way to deal with how you feel when life turns sour. A failed relationship. A fight with friends or family. A painful rejection. How do you deal with something like that? The truth is you don't need to answer that question. It's not your job or your responsibility. How can you answer something that cuts to the heart of you? You can't. Instead, take solace in the fact that life will carry you forward anyway. Let it.

You're part of the world and it's a big and powerful place. Just by living life, you'll move forward, past the pain, past the heartbreak. Immerse yourself in the necessities of your day. Keep your other friendships and relationships alive. Let your loved ones share and ease your burden. Shop. Work. Eat. These seem like simple points but they're daily milestones in your journey forward. Mark them quietly and don't look back. Look ahead and ask what new routes your life might take. Where might they lead you?

The Card Reversed

The Five of Cups reversed carries a message of forgiveness and a reminder that you're not alone. On the one hand, the card is talking about the forgiveness of others. Have you been carrying a burden or a secret or guilt that is weighing you down? You know you will feel better if you share your sorrows. Kept inside, they will poison you. You know better than that.

Reversed, the card can also be a sign that the time has come to forgive yourself, however. You cannot carry guilt for things you have said or done (or thought!) forever. You're imperfect, just like everyone else. Just because you don't see the mistakes others make doesn't mean they don't make them. They do. Just like you. And just like you would forgive others for their mistakes, you can forgive yourself as well. Let the pain go. You don't need it anymore.

Affirmation

I am imperfect. I am human.

Six of Cups

♥

It's called your happy place for a reason. An experience, a memory, a source of joy. You need to be able to draw from this well in times of need and fill it up in times of plenty. Take care of your happy place and it will take care of you. The Six of Cups are overflowing with just what you need to make it happen.

Common Portrayal

One child hands a cup filled with flowers to another child. Five other cups stand nearby, also filled with flowers, and in the distance, an adult walks away.

The Card Upright

The Six of Cups is about creating joy rather than waiting for it to come to you, and the card is pretty specific in its advice. It's telling you to rely on your partner and loved ones and build a special, shared space for you both where you can live joyous, loving lives. Set aside time to have fun together and make sure you make the most of that time. That's a key aspect of the card—this all takes effort. Don't just expect good things to come your way. You'll have to work for it. But it will be joyous work.

The card also stresses the importance of nurturing your inner child. The Sun in the Major Arcana addresses this as well, but with the Six of Cups, it's specifically focused on tapping into that more playful side of yourself as a route to happiness. You simply must keep that part of yourself alive and indulge in it regularly—it's nourishment for the soul. You can then take the enthusiasm and energy you create through intentional play and put it to use in your daily life, sharing that joy with your loved ones.

The Card Reversed

When reversed, the Six of Cups turns the inner child idea on its head and asks whether you're spending too much time dwelling on the past and not enough on where you are, or where you're going. It can be a fine balance, but you should let your intuition be your guide—if this card speaks to you during your reading, ask yourself whether there is something (or someone) you need to let go of in order to move on. Clinging to past loves and losses can prevent you from seeing what is right in front of you.

The card can also be a call to make peace with the past. Are you carrying around guilt for things you're ashamed of? Are you nurturing a grudge that isn't doing you any favors? Even if you don't act on it, thoughts of that nature can poison you. Ask yourself why you're still hanging onto them. What can you do to move past these negative feelings? What can others do to help you?

Affirmation

I know how to play. I know why it matters.

Seven of Cups

♥

It's great to have choices and even better if you have the imagination to take advantage of them. But not all choices are equal and just because you can imagine something, it doesn't mean you should try to make it come true. Take a sip from the Seven of Cups and give it some thought.

Common Portrayal

Seven cups are overflowing with all manner of wonders. A figure stands before them, unable to choose which cup to take.

The Card Upright

The Seven of Cups is a lesson in picking the correct path. Are you presented with a variety of options, but you can't decide which to take? Multiple suitors, jealous friends, and family, differing demands on your time—all of these require choices of you. It can be tempting to put off such choices and enjoy the luxury of indulging in all your options, but that can't last. So how do you choose?

The key is being able to discern fantasy from reality, being able to see each choice for what it truly is. A course of action that seems attractive on the surface can conceal hidden dangers. Do not ask yourself what is best. Instead, ask yourself what is true. What do the choices in your life actually mean to you on an emotional level? Is your desire for something or someone a symptom of something else? See your choices for what they truly are before deciding which path to walk.

The Card Reversed

The Seven of Cups reversed tells much the same tale as the upright version of the card, but with greater emphasis on the internal truth of the choices you make. It's asking you to be self-critical and ask yourself whether you're deceiving yourself. Have you allowed yourself to be misled by wishing for something that's never going to happen? Is it interfering with your happiness? You probably already know the answers to those questions.

The card can also speak to you when you're feeling over-whelmed by life and the choices it demands of you. It's a reminder that it's okay to step back and take a breath. You don't have to take on everything all at once. In fact, you don't have to take on anything at all. The Seven of Cups reversed tells you that you can refuse choices. You don't have to say "yes" to anything. Ever.

Affirmation

I see my true path. I own my choices.

Eight of Cups

♥

When the time comes to walk away, you'll know it. There's no shame in making a clean break—it's often the healthiest choice for all concerned—and there's no mistaking the feelings of relief and freedom that follow. The Eight of Cups are just the medicine for times like this.

Common Portrayal

Eight cups stand stacked, arranged as if one is missing. A figure leans on a staff as they walk away into the woods.

The Card Upright

The image on the card says it all—the figure can see that something is missing and has turned away as a result. The concept of something being missing is central to the Eight of Cups. The card is asking you to look at your current situation and consider whether you need more than what is before you. Is there something missing from your life? Can you describe what it is? What would it take to make you re-engage?

Sometimes the answer really is just to walk away, and the card is reassuring you that this is a valid choice. You aren't required to stick around in unhealthy or unpleasant relationships. If you've thought the matter through and there's nothing left for you to make you stay, then leaving is the correct decision. That same sense of what was missing from your life will be your guide on a new path that will take you where you need to go.

The Card Reversed

The Eight of Cups reversed can speak to the need to move on from a harmful situation, as with the upright version of the card. When it appears in your reading, the reversed card is underlining the need to make a final decision. If this card speaks to you, it's probably long past the time when you could fix things. Now you need to accept how things are or move on.

More often, the reversed Eight of Cups is a reminder to check in with yourself and make sure you aren't lingering in a relationship or friendship for longer than you should. Has the time come to make that clean break and you're just putting it off? For a while, that's okay but sooner or later, you need to make the move. The Eight of Cups reversed is like your "check engine" light, so pay attention when it crops up.

Affirmation

The time has come to leave. The time has come to begin again.

Nine of Cups

Achieving a goal you've longed for is a wonderful feeling. You're filled with a sense of your own accomplishments, and you feel like you're overflowing with love for the world. These feelings don't come along often enough, but the Nine of Cups hold a brew that will help bring them to life.

Common Portrayal

Nine cups are arrayed in splendor. A figure sits contentedly before them.

The Card Upright

The Nine of Cups is often called the Wish Card and with good reason. When it appears in your reading, it's a sign that you need to act on those things you desire most. A relationship. A friendship. Building or mending bridges between loved ones. You will know it in your heart when the time is right for this, and this card is telling you not to delay in pursuing what you most wish for. Ask yourself what you really want from your current (or future) relationship and decide how you will make it happen.

Achieving something you've been longing for is great and you should allow yourself the time to appreciate that. When we're starting new relationships, we put in a great deal of effort to be the best version of ourselves—but that shine can fade. They call it the "honeymoon period" for a reason. The Nine of Cups is a reminder not to just sit pretty and feel like your work is done. Relationships need continual work and the determination to see it through. Celebrate when you achieve relationship goals but pour the energy that gives you back into the relationship to sustain what you have achieved.

The Card Reversed

The Nine of Cups reversed often speaks to us during a reading when we should be feeling great, but we know deep down that something's not right. Everyone else is smiling so why aren't you? The card is telling you to look inside and see where that doubt is coming from. Are you concerned about your relationship or friendships? What is causing that concern? Is there something you or a loved one has said or done? What can you do to address those concerns? What *should* you do?

Similarly, the reversed card can also be asking you to look within for happiness and success, instead of seeking it in the world outside. Happiness starts inside us and grows there. The Nine of Cups reversed is asking what it would take for a seed of happiness to bud inside you. Do you need a relationship in order to be happy? What personal, private thing could you do that would bring you joy, even if you don't share it with anyone else?

Affirmation

I see my joy. I am its creator.

Ten of Cups

♥

Finding happiness in yourself, by yourself, is fulfilling indeed. But sharing that happiness with others in mutual love is where the magic really happens. It's how we're meant to live, and the Ten of Cups has the recipe for making it happen.

Common Portrayal

A rainbow bearing ten cups fills the sky. Below, parents watch their children playing happily.

The Card Upright

The Ten of Cups is as plain as its imagery. Happiness is found in sharing love with others. Usually, that starts with family, but not everyone has that kind of relationship with their family, so the card also encompasses found families.

When this card appears in your reading, ask yourself how you can draw on others, share your own joys and burdens with them, and share theirs in turn. Not all relationships need to be romantic, and the Ten of Cups is a reminder that you can find happiness and fulfillment in the bonds of family and deep friendship.

There's also a personal aspect to the Ten of Cups, which tells you to listen to your heart. When considering relationship choices, you should be cultivating honesty with yourself. With that kind of inner clarity, you can use your heart as a compass to help you choose relationships that are healthy and wholesome. What is your heart telling you? How can you use that insight to improve your relationships and love life?

The Card Reversed

When reversed, the Ten of Cups points to disharmony. While the upright card speaks of unity and shared love, the reversed card suggests that you may be experiencing conflict with those closest to you. When this card speaks to you, ask yourself whether there are rifts you can heal or bridges you can rebuild. What would you need to do to set matters right? What would the other person need to do? Can you tell them?

Internally, the Ten of Cups reversed can be a call to focus more on those close to you, and a suggestion that you may have been neglecting those bonds. Have you been overly focused on career achievements, to the detriment of your home life? Do you need to spend more time with your friends or family? Have you been shutting yourself off from the world? If so, why? What would need to happen to make you want to engage more with those around you?

Affirmation

In others, I find love. They find love in me.

Page of Cups

Being open to new ideas is important, but even more important is seeking them out. Don't sit around waiting for the excitement to come your way. Get out there and hunt those experiences down. The Page of Cups is more than happy to lend a hand.

Common Portrayal

A gaudily clad individual holds a single cup. The head of a fish pokes out of the cup.

The Card Upright

Like the other Page cards, the Page of Cups is about exploring something new. In the case of this card, it's focused on your creative strengths and your emotional inner life. The card serves as a reminder to play to those strengths when building new relationships with the people around you, but also to listen closely to your feelings. When meeting someone new or embarking on a new phase in your life, your gut instinct can be a powerful tool until you get a sense of the lie of the land.

Use that intuition to seek out people, friendships, and partners who move you and inspire you. If you're struggling with the relationships in your life, consider them from a purely emotional angle. Is there a new perspective there that can give you insight into how to move forward? Is there a way you can apply a creative solution to the problem, something that feels like it comes out of left field? Try to approach your issue on an intuitive level and see what fresh ideas that spark.

The Card Reversed

The Page of Cups reversed also speaks to creativity but it's asking whether you need to be sharing your creative and intuitive powers with others. Is your gut telling you something that you don't want to hear? Can you see a way to solve a problem in your life but you're not sure if you should speak up? The time comes when your ideas will find their mark. Ask yourself whether that time has come.

When reversed, the card is also a warning to keep your emotional side in check and not let your gut rule your head. The Tarot talks about balance fairly often and that's front and center here—success in life and love comes from having a balanced approach. Balance your emotions with a cooler head. Let your insight guide your more analytical ways of thinking but always maintain a balance.

Affirmation

I hear my heart. I heed its guidance.

Knight of Cups

♥

There's nothing wrong with being a hopeless romantic or wearing your heart on your sleeve. Far better to be open and honest about who you are than hide behind a mask. Mount up and let the Knight of Cups lead the way.

Common Portrayal

A mounted knight in a winged helm and boots holds a single cup. Images of fish adorn his clothing.

The Card Upright

The Knight of Cups is one of the most romantic cards in your reading. It's asking you to share your emotions and your passions, to be open and bold, to ride forth and proclaim yourself to the world. The card is a reminder that you can't be faint-hearted when it comes to your passions. Let your emotions speak clearly and plainly. Don't let them rule you but don't hide them. They are your banner—let them fly!

The more chivalrous aspect of the card reminds you to consider the emotions and passions of others. Like a classical knight who defends the weak, are there ways you can protect and nurture others, so they can embrace their own true feelings and desires? If you were in the other person's shoes, ask what one thing you would most wish for—perhaps you can be the knight who rides to the rescue to provide it!

The Card Reversed

The Knight of Cups reversed is all about keeping those emotions in check. On the one hand, the card focuses on negative emotions and asks whether your current situation is being influenced by your own negativity. Are you grumpy, sulky, or out of sorts with someone close to you? Are you maybe just overreacting a teensy little bit? Might it not be better to take a breath and find a way to mend bridges?

The reversed card also has advice for your inner life as well. It's asking you to check whether you've let yourself be carried away by emotionally driven fantasies or allowed yourself to indulge too deeply in an obsession or other deep fascination. When this card speaks to you, ask yourself whether you need to clear your head, take a step back, and maybe ease off a little.

Affirmation

My arms and armor are love. These weapons defeat all.

Queen of Cups

♥

When you're there for others—really there for them—you build around yourself a world driven by love. Nurturing, caring, and compassionate, you can find yourself surrounded by people who come to honor and respect you. Let the Queen of Cups show you how to bring them into your life.

Common Portrayal

A queen sits on an ornate throne holding a sealed cup. The throne and her robes are decorated with aquatic designs.

The Card Upright

The Queen of Cups is a call to take your nurturing instincts and use them to help those around you. That's really all there is to it. Ask yourself how you can help those nearest and dearest to you, particularly on an emotional level. Can you be there for them as a shoulder to cry on, a stabilizing influence, or just someone who will hold space for them? This kind of support is at the heart of all successful relationships.

Don't be afraid to take the lead here either. You can step up and be a guiding force in the lives of your loved ones. When people are emotionally vulnerable, they often can't think straight or even cope with day-to-day life. Can you be that zone of calm or source of emotional strength? If you can cultivate this approach as part of your life, you'll find yourself spreading peace and love just by your presence.

The Card Reversed

The Queen of Cups reversed is a warning to not let yourself drown in the drama of others. Helping those in need is one thing. Getting drawn into needless emotional nonsense is another. Your life is not a blank slate for someone else to scrawl their emotional problems all over. Like the regal queen, know when to turn people like that down. You do not need to grant them an audience, your majesty.

As an extension of that, the card can also be a call to check in on yourself. If you've been spending lots of time helping others, don't let yourself burn out. When your loved ones are in genuine need, you're there for them, of course—but you also need to take time to recharge so you can continue to help others. You're no good to anyone if you use up every last bit of energy and leave nothing for yourself.

Affirmation

Love is the whole of the law. I preach it gladly.

King of Cups

♥

Your emotions are powerful tools. Harnessed, they can carry you places that simple determination cannot. Uncontrolled, they can destroy your life. When in balance with your more rational side, there is little that can stand in your way. Prepare to rule with the King of Cups!

Common Portrayal

A king sits enthroned, holding a cup in one hand and his rod of office in the other. Aquatic symbols adorn his robes and thrones alike.

The Card Upright

The King of Cups asks you to reach for your highest emotional ideals and live by them in order to achieve the highest happiness. It presumes you're ready to balance your emotions and your rational mind in how you approach your relationships. Like a regal monarch of old, you must be even-handed, clear-headed, and compassionate in order to make the most of your love life, your connections to your friends, and your bonds with your family.

Notably, the card doesn't talk about abandoning your emotions—this is still the suit of Cups, after all! Instead, it's asking you to at last find that balance that allows you to tap into your emotions when you need them without letting them overwhelm you, and to use them alongside more rational thinking in order to build strong and lasting relationships. That kind of inner harmony is deeply attractive and makes you a desirable choice for a partner. There's nothing more compelling than someone in tune with their feelings who knows how to make use of those inner drives.

The Card Reversed

We've talked above about how your emotions make powerful tools for dealing with your loved ones—it should come as no surprise to you that they make devastating weapons. If you've ever completely lost your temper with someone you care about, torn strips off them, only to cool down later, you'll know how horrible it feels when you realize what you've done. The King of Cups reversed is a giant neon sign warning you about that kind of behavior.

Like a ruler who has become too powerful, your emotions can take over and turn you into a bit of a monster. If this card is speaking to you during your reading, ask yourself if you've gone too far recently with someone close to you. Do you need to make amends? How would you do so in the most gracious, compassionate way possible? Ask yourself how that might improve your relationships with the people you value most.

Affirmation

I rule my heart. My rule is just.

Suit of Swords

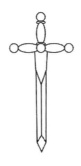

Ace of Swords

♥

A sharp mind is an attractive mind and there are few better ways to sharpen your mind than by trying something new. That fresh rush of experience fills you with excitement and energy, making you immediately stand out. Draw the Ace of Swords and see how you can put that beautiful mind of yours to use!

Common Portrayal

A hand emerges from a cloud, wielding a single sword. The blade is crowned, with the crown itself bearing a wreath.

The Card Upright

Like the other Aces, this card is about new beginnings—but because we're looking at the suit of Swords, we know that the card is about our thoughts, our intellect.

So, the Ace of Swords is asking you to think clearly when embarking on a new relationship or friendship, or when a loved one asks you for something or suggests a course of action. You shouldn't shut your emotions out entirely, but this card does suggest that you should be as rational as you can be when thinking about how to proceed.

People will try to play on your emotions and this card is a good reminder to be wary of those who do. You don't need that kind of influence in your life. But because this is the suit of Swords, the card is also double-edged. It's telling you to think carefully about how you speak to and treat your loved ones. Careless words can hurt the people you love, so keep a clear head and think before you speak.

The Card Reversed

The Ace of Swords reversed can be a tough card to deal with when it appears in your reading, because it's a sharp warning to step back and reconsider. Have you been having second thoughts about a new relationship or even an existing one? Has your partner's behavior raised questions for you? If so, good! You should question what goes on around you, particularly where your love life is concerned. Don't let anyone walk all over you.

This can be hard advice to take, particularly if your heart is all fired up and you're ready to leap into something new with someone exciting! Remember that one of the key lessons of the Tarot is balance. You simply must balance your heart with your head, particularly when you're in that honeymoon phase. And if you feel unsure about things afterwards, ask yourself why. What is it about your current relationship that makes you reconsider after thinking it through? What can you do to banish your doubts?

Affirmation

I begin with a clear mind. It shows me the road to love.

Two of Swords

♥

Life is confusing enough without adding love into the bargain. Love stops you from thinking straight, makes you behave like an idiot, and generally complicates everything. Unfortunately, we're kind of stuck with it. Wield the Two of Swords to cut through the confusion and find the way forward.

Common Portrayal

A figure sits blindfolded, a sword in each hand. In the background, islands dot a large body of water.

The Card Upright

The Two of Swords seems like a difficult card to process on the surface, but it's quite straightforward. The card is a call to examine your existing situation carefully—your relationship, your friendship, your connection to your family—and ask yourself if you have the full picture. When we're struggling to make sense of relationship problems, it can often be because we aren't seeing things clearly. Like the figure on the card, you're blindfolded. You need to remove that blindfold in order to see clearly.

So, if this card speaks out to you during your reading, ask yourself whether you feel like you're missing something. Are you in conflict with your partner but you can't figure out why? Are your friends or family upset with you for no apparent reason? Communicate clearly and honestly and ask for the same in return, figuratively ripping the blindfold from your eyes. Before you react, consider whether you have all the information.

The Card Reversed

The Two of Swords reversed carries many of the same messages as the upright version of the card, but they are focused inwards. In other words, the card is a warning against self-deception. Are you being honest with yourself about what you want from your relationships? Are you refusing to acknowledge problems in your love life, or even in your partner? As tempting as it might be to stick your head in the sand, doing so will not end well. Relationships are built on honesty, and the first person you need to be honest with is yourself.

The reversed card can also be of value if you feel like you're stuck in a rut, or you've reached some kind of impasse with your loved ones. Like removing the blindfold, the card is suggesting you take a fresh look at your relationships and see if you can find a different way to communicate your needs or gain new insight into the needs of your friends, family, or partner. Try to keep a clear head and view the matter from the perspective of those close to you. What might they ask of you? Can you give it?

Affirmation

I see the truth. I accept it.

Three of Swords

♥

Love hurts and there's no escaping that fact. And when you're hurting, the last thing you want to hear is that you need to find a silver lining to help you through. But that's exactly what this card is about. So let the Three of Swords point the way to a kinder future.

Common Portrayal

Three swords pierce a heart. In the background, storm clouds gather.

The Card Upright

The Three of Swords is all about exactly what it looks like—being stabbed through the heart. Discovering that your special someone has been cheating on you. Finding out that the object of your desire has no interest in you whatsoever. Taking a swing at a relationship and striking out, again and again. How do you cope? Well, the simple answer is that you don't have to. Sometimes screaming your frustrations at the sky (or into a pillow) is the correct response.

When the agony begins to pass—and it will—you can take a breath and start to assess your situation. Pain is a great teacher because it teaches us to avoid being hurt in the same way again. Ask yourself what you can do in the future to avoid that kind of pain. Do you need to be more realistic about who you set your sights on? Or less sensitive to the opinions of others? Having a big heart can be wonderful, but it can also leave you open to emotional abuse. Protect yourself.

The Card Reversed

The Three of Swords reversed is a personal card that speaks to your internal thought processes. It specifically speaks to your inner critic and asks whether you're showing the sort of love to yourself that you expect from others—and which you presumably also show to others. It's important to build loving relationships with the people around you, but don't forget that you're people too. You must learn to love yourself.

Many people struggle with this because we have such strong inner voices. But these inner voices can be overly critical. Are you being too hard on yourself? When you criticize yourself, ask whether you'd criticize a loved one in the same way. If not, then why on Earth would you speak to yourself that way? Love flows inwards as well as outwards, never forget that.

Affirmation

My wounds are my teachers. I hear them.

Four of Swords

♥

Love can wait. It's not going anywhere and sometimes you need a break from all the drama and the heartache and the late-night texting. Instead, kick back, relax, and let your inner world recharge. The Four of Swords will guard you while you rest.

Common Portrayal

A knight lies in final rest atop a tomb. A sword adorns the tomb, while three others hang above.

The Card Upright

The Four of Swords is a call to step back from the struggles of your love life and spend time alone, recharging your batteries. It's a classic Swords card in that it's telling you to let your head lead the way while your heart gets to hush for a while. The demands of your emotions can be very draining and that can interfere with your ability to make good decisions about your relationships. Step away, let your emotions settle, and assess with a clear head.

Seclusion is a key element of this card—you really do need to put some distance between yourself and your loved ones, if only for a while. If you've been arguing with your partner, it's perfectly fine to ask for some space to get your head straight. Similarly, if you're feeling overwhelmed by the situation in your love life, no one will think badly of you if you need to disconnect from the world for a few days.

The Card Reversed

The Four of Swords reversed carries a similar message to the upright version of the card, but it's angled far more sharply. If this card is speaking to you during your reading, ask yourself whether you've been neglecting your own self-care for too long. Particularly when you're in the honeymoon phase of a relationship, it's easy to overlook issues that you might otherwise pick up on. Have you been ignoring something that's actually bothering you about your relationship or loved ones? Do you need to step back in order to process things so you can know how to behave? Make sure you listen to this warning—the alternative is burnout.

When reversed, the card can also be asking you to examine frustrations with your love life more deeply. Under this aspect of the card, you're not just taking a step back to recharge, but you're taking the time to reassess your entire relationship. Examine your concerns from top to bottom. The card doesn't need to point you towards a separation (although don't be afraid to ask for some time away if you need it) but it does want you to have an honest conversation with yourself about what you want in your love life.

Affirmation

I am renewed. My thoughts are unclouded now.

Five of Swords

♥

So, you've delivered the perfect cutting retort, silencing your opponent. Maybe you even made them cry. Great. Now what? Unlike in the movies, you can't skip to the next scene after a bad fight. Life goes on, dragging you along with it. So, sheath your blades and let the Five of Swords show you how to find peace after conflict.

Common Portrayal

A figure gathers fallen swords. Nearby, two others walk away, heads downcast.

The Card Upright

In Tarot, the number five symbolizes conflict, and the Five of Swords does not disappoint. The card carries advice that is both general and specific. On the general level, the

Five of Swords tells you to choose your fights carefully. Relationships are about compromises and not everything will go your way. Instead of pushing back at every little thing you don't like, pick those issues that matter most and address those with your special someone.

If it does come to a conflict, you might find yourself on the receiving end and you might equally be dishing it out. You won't have a love life that's free of arguments, so you need to learn how to defuse them. The quickest route to this is to apologize. You should never say you're sorry when you aren't in the wrong, of course, but if you've hurt somcone, can you find it in yourself to make a real and sincere apology? If you can't, ask yourself why not? What would need to change for you to be able to build bridges again?

The Card Reversed

The Five of Swords reversed poses an interesting question—what if there's no point to arguing? Some disagreements in relationships just go around and around with no resolution. These can be long-term too, resurfacing after years. If you find yourself caught up in an argument with your loved ones that just doesn't seem to end, ask yourself whether it would be better to just step away. What would you actually lose if you just let it go?

On a more positive note, the reversed version of the card can also be a suggestion to take the energies created during conflict and use them. If you've had a big clash with your partner, you may find that this has actually cleared the air, allowing you to make some long-needed changes. Or perhaps you've drawn a line under a bad relationship—what can you take from it to make the most of being single again?

Affirmation

I only fight when I must. I always apologize when I should.

Six of Swords

♥

You'll find yourself carrying plenty of burdens in life, so you need to figure out when it's time to set some of them aside and focus on yourself. The journey will be much easier if you do. The Six of Swords stand ready to teach you how.

Common Portrayal

A figure ferries a parent and child across a river in a boat. Six swords stand in the prow of the vessel.

The Card Upright

When the Six of Swords appears in your reading, you can breathe a sigh of relief. This card is asking whether you've taken on more than you should. Is it time to let go? A former lover. An old rival. A disloyal ex. All these and more can prey on your mind, casting their shadow over your current relationship and interfering with your love life. The Six of Swords is a reminder that you can let these burdens go.

Simply put, you're better off without this emotional baggage. You don't want to be that date who can't shut up about their ex, or someone who is unable to trust a new partner because of what an old one did. Carrying these issues around isn't just an internal issue—they manifest in the world around you too.

The Card Reversed

When reversed, the Six of Swords is speaking to you about a rite of passage—a struggle you must endure in order to achieve what you want. In terms of your relationships, this can be unpleasant—a revelation about a partner, a protracted divorce—or it can be more positive—the struggle to win the attention of your special someone, working hard to forge a new friendship. Whatever the case, the card is telling you that it's worth sticking it out. When you come out on the other side, you'll be stronger and wiser.

If you're struggling to move on from a painful breakup or other problem in your relationship, the Six of Swords reversed is also a reminder to ask yourself whether you have any unfinished business that's holding you back. Do you need to have some final words with an ex to find closure? Do you owe someone an apology? What would it take for you to be able to put these problems to bed and move on to a happier place in your love life?

Affirmation

This is not my burden. These are not my responsibilities.

Seven of Swords

♥

There are those who claim that the Eleventh Commandment is "thou shalt not get caught" and maybe they're right. Problem is, everyone gets caught sooner or later. Your secrets won't stay secret forever, and your sins will most definitely find you out. Unsheathe the Seven of Swords and prepare for what's coming your way.

Common Portrayal

A figure carries five swords away from a large encampment. Two other swords stand nearby.

The Card Upright

So, the Seven of Swords is about honesty. Or, more specifically, dishonesty and its consequences. This can include times when you've been lied to by a loved one or deceived by your partner, but it applies equally to those times when you aren't being honest yourself. Unsurprisingly, the card paints this as less than ideal. You shouldn't be lying to your loved ones and nor should you accept that kind of behavior from them.

But there's another interesting side to the card, and that's one of strategy—which is a polite way of saying being sneaky for a good reason. Honesty is important but you must also protect yourself and those close to you. A loved one may ask you to keep potentially hurtful confidence about a mutual friend—one you decide to respect. If you find your partner is being abusive, you absolutely do not have to open yourself up to further pain. Outright honesty at all times can sometimes be a poor strategic choice. This card is asking you to make sure you think through the consequences of speaking openly—or remaining silent.

The Card Reversed

When reversed, the Seven of Swords can be asking you to be more honest with yourself. Are there elements in your relationship that are upsetting you, but you aren't facing up to them? Wherever this self-deception is coming from, the card is asking you to examine the issue more honestly. Not only is this self-deception holding you back, but it affects how you interact with your loved ones on a subconscious level, harming your relationships.

There's a powerful aspect to this side of the card that's often neglected. Because at its heart, the Seven of Swords reversed is telling you to believe in yourself. Your true self. Don't tell yourself that you're not good enough for someone. You are. Don't tell yourself that you're not strong enough to walk away from a bad relationship. You are. Don't tell yourself that you can't find the kind of love that you're looking for. You absolutely can. Self-doubt is a lie.

Affirmation

I face the truth. I face myself.

Eight of Swords

♥

You can be your own worst enemy. We all can. It's just how we're wired. But that doesn't make it any less frustrating when we talk ourselves into some ridiculous situation or other or talk ourselves out of one that was perfectly fine. Thankfully, the Eight of Swords is here to cut through all the confusion and set you on the right path.

Common Portrayal

A woman stands tied and blindfolded. Eight swords stand guard around her.

The Card Upright

The Eight of Swords carries strong words about freedom. It's specifically referring to freedom from chains you create yourself. In relationships, these often show up as choosing the wrong type of partner over and over, allowing people close to you to walk all over you, not speaking up when you should, and the like. Although situations like this can come about because of others, at the end of the day, the responsibility for them lies with you. You hold the key to chains you've made yourself.

That's the essence of the Eight of Swords—you put yourself where you are, so you're the one to fix the problem. Recognizing this as the issue is a real hurdle, but if this card is speaking to you strongly from your reading, you should take it as a sign to think carefully about how you're treating yourself and how you're letting others treat you. Relationships require mutual respect. You must respect yourself and you must demand respect from your loved ones as well—just as you respect them in turn.

The Card Reversed

The Eight of Swords reversed reinforces the message of the upright card but concentrates more closely on your inner world and how you treat and value yourself. Being overly critical of yourself limits you. You must never forget the central message of the Tarot, which is to love yourself and to make yourself into someone you can love. From that place of self-love, let go of habits and beliefs, and ideas that only hold you back. See the goodness in yourself and free yourself from unhealthy thoughts.

This self-love will have an immediate effect on your relationships with other people. Freed from negative thought processes, you will become a more fulfilled and happier person and your loved ones will notice. It's not rocket science—happier people are more attractive and better able to build loving relationships. The Eight of Swords reversed is a reminder to let yourself be the best version of yourself that you can be.

Affirmation

I made these chains. They are mine to break.

Nine of Swords

♥

Just because you're paranoid, doesn't mean they aren't out to get you. Except when it does. Although how would you know? And that right there is the problem with letting your imagination run riot—once you start, you're kind of stuck with it. But fear not! The Nine of Swords is here to drive away the darkness!

Common Portrayal

A figure sits upright in bed, face in hands. Nine swords float above the bed.

The Card Upright

The Nine of Swords is actually deeply loving and positive, despite its appearance. It's a reminder that many of our fears and concerns about our love lives come from our own imagination. You can imagine, no doubt, how developing fears that your partner is being unfaithful could become a self-fulfilling prophecy. Similarly, treating your friends poorly because you imagine them to be gossiping about you will lead to the thing you fear.

So, the Nine of Swords is a reminder to let these imaginations remain where they belong. Better still, talk them over with the people concerned. Why might you be worrying about your partner's fidelity? Is there something you need to talk to them about? Do you feel like you've drifted apart from your friends? Is there something you could do about that? Don't be like the person on the card, up at night with worry. Ask yourself why you're dwelling on these fears. What would it take for you to feel more relaxed?

The Card Reversed

The Nine of Swords reversed focuses your attention inwards, applying the lessons of the upright card to your relationship with yourself in another reminder of the importance of self-love. As a Swords card, it's stressing the importance of avoiding negative thinking. But its position is a clue to its deeper meaning. In the Tarot, Nines often signifies the final step before completing a journey, and here the Nine of Swords reversed is asking you what is holding you back from completing yours.

If this card is speaking to you, ask yourself what you could do to improve your chances of finding the kind of love you're looking for. Do you feel ready for a serious relationship, but something is in the way? Are you trying to improve your current relationship, but something isn't quite right? What could you do in the privacy of your own mind that would help you move forward? Are you all that's holding yourself back?

Affirmation

I face my fear. It passes through me.

Ten of Swords

♥

All good things come to an end. Thankfully, so do all bad things. Even when something unpleasant is over, it can take time to adjust and figure out what the shape of your new life is. The Ten of Swords will help you carve that life into the shape you need.

Common Portrayal

A figure lies face down, impaled by ten swords. The figure is draped in cloth.

The Card Upright

Don't be alarmed by the image on the card—no one is getting stabbed, even if it feels like it. That's just how endings feel, and the Ten of Swords is all about endings. When relationships end, it is never pleasant, even if you're the one doing the ending. And it's even worse when you're on the receiving end. The Ten of Swords is a reminder to keep a clear head at times like that because you're on the verge of something new and you don't want to miss the opportunity to make the most of it.

The card instead tells you to balance your emotions with clear thinking. Set aside time to process what you're going through so you aren't caught up in the heat of things. This applies doubly if you're the one calling the shots—maybe you're ending the relationship, stepping away from a friend, cutting off a family member—because you need to remain level-headed in order to find true closure.

The Card Reversed

When reversed, the Ten of Swords is asking you whether you're ready for the changes happening around you. If this card is speaking to you strongly, it may be because you're confronted with a big change in your relationships, and you're absolutely not ready to deal with it. The sense of shock and fear that accompanies a situation like that can be paralyzing.

At times like that, the card's advice is to step back and reassess the situation. As with the upright card, take actual time and space for yourself so you can think clearly and figure out what is upsetting you. What is it about changes to your relationship or love life that are causing you concern and stopping you from moving forward? What would have to happen to change this for you? And what can you do to help that change take place?

Affirmation

I see the future. I welcome it with a clear head.

Page of Swords

♥

You've heard the expression "change your mind" but have you ever *really* tried to change your mind? Not just your opinions about something, but the actual way you think about things? The Page of Swords has some suggestions about how you might try.

Common Portrayal

A page looks off into the distance while holding a single sword. Clouds dot the heavens in the background.

The Card Upright

The Page of Swords is about new ways of thinking. How we experience our relationships is very much determined by how we think. If you're an optimistic person by nature, you'll see your love life differently than someone who has a less positive outlook. If you change your outlook, it will affect how happy you are. And how much others want to be around you, which is the core of all relationships.

A trick to understanding the way you experience your relationships is to always ask yourself *why*. When you encounter a problem in your love life and you feel like you might have been partly responsible, ask yourself why that was. Can you trace it back to thoughts you had? Why were you thinking those things? What can you do to improve how your own thoughts affect your relationships?

The Card Reversed

The Page of Swords reversed is a call to share your thoughts with the people around you. Just as the upright version of the card addresses how your thoughts can affect your relationships, the reversed version of the card is all but insisting that you let this happen. Is there something you've been longing to say to your partner, but you haven't had the courage? The Page of Swords reversed tells you not to be shy—speak your mind!

The reversed card can also carry a warning to think ahead. If you're intending on speaking up to someone close to you about a sensitive topic, take a few minutes to plan out how you want to bring your point across. You should still speak your truth but be mindful of the feelings of those close to you. Relationships need mutual respect, so show as much respect as you would expect to receive from those you care about.

Affirmation

I know myself. I know I can change.

Knight of Swords

♥

You know what you want and you're certain it's right for you. That's an empowering feeling and worth pursuing. Don't let people stand in your way—the time has come for you to claim what is yours. Ready your blade to do battle alongside the Knight of Swords!

Common Portrayal

An armored knight on a white horse charges forward. A sword is upheld in his hand.

The Card Upright

The Knight of Swords is a card that charges into your life, upends everything, then charges off again. As a Swords card, it's asking you to think clearly about what you want in love and in a relationship, and then to simply get out there and take it. Or at the very least try. This card is a call to action, to take charge of your love life, to state clearly and loudly what you need from your partner, and not to let anyone else tell you otherwise.

Because it's a Swords card, of course, the Knight requires some forethought. Don't rush in blindly—as noted above, you need to have your thinking cap on—but plan in advance how you're going to approach things. Rather than blurting out your ideas to your partner, try making a list first. Don't just demand things from your loved ones—make sure you can explain your needs and you'll find them more ready to accept and support you. Clarity and communication will bring the results you desire.

The Card Reversed

The Knight of Swords reversed emphasizes the need to think through matters of the heart before charging ahead and trying to change everything. When the reversed version of the card appears in your reading, ask yourself whether you're clear about your intentions and desires where your relationships are concerned. You can't communicate your needs to your partner if you haven't set them out clearly for yourself. Are there areas in your love life that you want to change?

The reversed version of the card can also be a suggestion that you aren't ready to share your needs yet. You may be able to explain what you're looking for in love, but are you ready to give back to another person what they need? The Knight of Swords reversed is asking whether you should spend a little more time working on how you express yourself with those close to you before being open to a relationship.

Affirmation

My time is now. My place is here.

Queen of Swords

♥

Knowing yourself and being honest about who you are is both liberating and empowering. Your truth is inescapable—no one can doubt you and people turn to you for advice. This is your hour. Come join the Queen of Swords on her throne.

Common Portrayal

A queen sits enthroned, cherubs and butterflies adorning her throne and robe. She holds a single sword in her hand.

The Card Upright

The Queen of Swords is a demanding card that calls on you to reach for your highest ideals, in yourself as much as in your relationships. The card asks you to have an open heart in all your relationships, from friends to lovers, accepting them for who they are, but maintaining a cool head at all times. Can you appreciate the depth and passion of your special someone without losing your composure? Your loved ones will come to appreciate you all the more.

Your emotions can cloud your judgment. When you're ready—honest with yourself, in tune with your needs, and open to the world—you can set those emotions aside and assess your situation clearly. This can be a powerful tool to uncover the reasons behind stress in your love life, allow you to figure out why you and your special someone are out of sync or see something you missed in any of your relationships. You can let your passions return when the time is right. For now, let clarity rule.

The Card Reversed

When reversed, the Queen of Swords carries two messages. Firstly, the card acts as a counterbalance to the upright version of the card. When maintaining clarity in order to assess your relationships and love life, you must take care not to allow yourself to become too aloof. If you're too distant, you risk damage to your relationships. This advice applies even when you aren't trying to keep a cool head about matters—don't squander the closeness that love of-fers.

Secondly, the Queen of Swords reversed asks you to make sure you aren't being unduly influenced by others. It can be hard to spot when those you love are exerting pres-sure on you so take a moment to ensure you aren't being nudged by an over-eager friend, relative, or lover. Like a queen, you should not bow to the desires of others unless you wish it yourself. Keep your mind clear of unwelcome influences.

Affirmation

I see the truth. I am the truth.

King of Swords

♥

When you remain true to yourself and those you love, a subtle transformation takes place. Peace, contentment, and a deep sense of knowing your place in life fills you. This is how it feels to be home. Come—the King of Swords has prepared a place for you at his table.

Common Portrayal

A king sits upon his throne, his rich robes flowing about him. He holds a sword in his hand.

The Card Upright

The King of Swords is a powerful card that promises real fulfillment in your love life. It asks you to know when to hold your emotions in check, to know how to assess yourself and your relationship with clarity, to deal with your loved ones fairly and honestly, and to speak your mind openly and with courage. And it doesn't just suggest this as an approach to dealing with current issues in your relationship—it suggests it as a way of living.

Beyond your current situation, the King of Swords is asking whether this is how you want to be in your love life on a permanent basis. The benefits of this are obvious—the happier and more secure you are in yourself, the happier you will be in love (and the happier your loved ones will be when they're with you!). As the highest card of the Swords suits, the King of Swords asks for a continual presence of mind but promises rewards that are simply regal.

The Card Reversed

When reversed, the King of Swords continues to be a positive but demanding card, and it continues to speak to your power. Ultimately, that's what the card is describing—the importance of having a strong mind as a way of finding happiness in love. When reversed, that power is quiet. Internal. The card is telling you that you can achieve your goals through subtle shows of strength rather than overt displays.

The mind is a powerful aphrodisiac, so when trying to draw the attention of that special someone, use your intellect and insight to spark fascinating conversations. Come up with unexpected date ideas. Surprise your partner with a gift that shows how deeply you understand them. You won't need to proclaim your feelings in a showy manner. Your quiet actions will show how much you understand the person you care about.

Affirmation

My mind is filled with love. It illuminates everything I do.

Suit of Pentacles

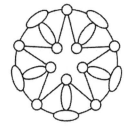

Ace of Pentacles

♥

When you feel something in your gut, you know it's the real deal. That physical sensation is like a confirmation of your emotions and instincts that tells you "This way!" so listen to what it's telling you. The Ace of Pentacles will make sure you're paying attention.

Common Portrayal

A hand holding a pentacle emerges from a cloud. Below, a hedged garden awaits.

The Card Upright

Aces govern beginnings and Pentacles deal with earthly, physical matters, so when this card appears in your reading, you could be in for a good time! Let's be honest, physical pleasure is part of love—for many of us, it's one of the most important parts of a relationship and even more so for shorter flings. The Ace of Pentacles is a reminder of the importance of the physical side of things. Don't be ashamed of prioritizing your own pleasure. Communicate your wants and needs clearly and respectfully. This allows you and your new partner to enjoy yourselves safely.

The card carries more earthy messages as well. The physical side of a relationship also involves questions such as where will you live—your place or your partner's? Somewhere shared? What about finances? Will you share a bank account? All these mundane questions form part and parcel of more serious relationships. The Ace of Pentacles is a call to give time to consider them when you're starting out with someone new.

The Card Reversed

The Ace of Pentacles reversed deepens the message of the upright version of the card, asking you to consider carefully your needs before embarking on a new relationship (or fling!). The card wants you to be sure that you've examined and communicated all your needs openly and honestly to yourself before you even consider talking to someone else about things. And if this card speaks to you strongly during your reading, that may be because you have questions to answer for yourself.

So, consider carefully whether you're ready to move in with a partner, for example. If you did, how much would your life change? Are you ready for that? And if you're considering taking your relationship to a more intimate physical level, check in with yourself and make sure you're completely comfortable with the idea. The Ace of Pentacles reversed is a reminder to ensure you're internally prepared before manifesting your desires in the external, physical world.

Affirmation

I know my needs. I ensure I meet them.

Two of Pentacles

♥

Are you sure you're juggling enough social commitments? Would you be happier if you added another couple of appointments, two more date nights, and a trip to see your family into the bargain? No? With the Two of Pentacles, you already have your hands full.

Common Portrayal

A figure juggles a pair of pentacles. The infinity sign loops around them both.

The Card Upright

The Two of Pentacles highlights a challenge that you're already aware of—there isn't enough time in the day (or night) for all the things you want to do. This card is just a little reminder to make sure you aren't over-extending yourself. Because if you start making appointments you can't keep, missing dates, and letting your friends and family down, you'll soon see the drawbacks to being too much of a social butterfly.

Instead, the card advises balance. Like the juggler on the card who is keeping both pentacles aloft, you need to make sure your relationships and social life are in balance. This goes double for your love life. Only commit to engagements you're sure you can attend. When you're better able to balance your social activities, you're better able to appreciate and enjoy those activities.

The Card Reversed

Reversed, the Two of Pentacles underlines the message of the upright version of the card and adds the consideration that you may be overlooking the needs of your loved ones because you're too busy or otherwise occupied. With the reversed card, it's not just about juggling too many commitments. It's a warning that spreading yourself too thin can actually cause problems for your loved ones.

If you've been juggling work and social engagements, you may have been neglecting your partner or family at a time when they really need you. If you've been throwing your-self into your new relationship, have you forgotten about your friends who were there for you when you were single? Not keeping on top of your social and relationship oblig-ations can cause real problems for you and those you care about. The Two of Pentacles reversed is a call to stop and check that you're taking this all into account.

Affirmation

I choose my obligations. I own them.

Three of Pentacles

♥

Don't try to go it alone. There's no need. You're surrounded by people who love you and value you, and they want to be part of your journey as well. With their help, you'll be able to travel much further than you thought. The Three of Pentacles will lead the way.

Common Portrayal

A mason and architects cooperate on building a cathedral. Above them, three pentacles are etched into the stone.

The Card Upright

Cooperation is the name of the game for the Three of Pentacles. It's the essence of any relationship—learning to get along with someone else for mutual benefit. It's why we do it. When this card appears in your reading, it's a suggestion to lean on those close to you for help in the real world. Their support doesn't just have to be emotional—you can ask friends, family, and loved ones for actual material help as well.

This can be something as simple as getting your partner to help out with groceries or chores around the house to more involved tasks like corralling all your friends to help you move house or planning a surprise party for someone. It can even mean borrowing money in times of crisis. Just because these subjects aren't passionate and romantic, doesn't mean that they aren't at the heart of all solid relationships. The Suit of Pentacles is firmly rooted in the real world and this card asks you to do the same.

The Card Reversed

The Three of Pentacles reversed presents an interesting contrast with the upright version of the card. On the one hand, it's asking you to look at your current relationship issues (including a lack of one). How much are these down to you not being in harmony with the needs of your loved ones? Or down to them not being in harmony with yours? Is there a way you can reach a compromise with the people involved to improve your relationships with them?

On the other hand, the card carries the suggestion that maybe you don't need to be cooperating with anyone. Maybe you can actually just go it alone. In the context of your love life, of course, this could mean that being single is the best choice for you right now. But it can also mean that it's okay to keep friends and family—and even your partner—at arm's length for a while. You need your space from time to time and the Three of Pentacles reversed is a reminder that you're within your rights to take it.

Affirmation

I am many. We are one.

Four of Pentacles

♥

Let's talk about green-eyed monsters for a moment. You know the one I mean. Jealousy rears its head more often than we'd like to admit and many of the things we do are motivated by a desire to be just a bit different. That's not always an unhealthy urge, though. The Four of Pentacles will show you how to find the right balance.

Common Portrayal

A figure sits cradling a pentacle. Two more lie beneath the figure's feet, with a fourth balanced atop their head.

The Card Upright

The Four of Pentacles is a reminder to remember where your true wealth lies. It's very tempting to look at others and feel jealous or to wish we had a different life. That can be a positive urge—seeing others happy in their relationships can prompt you to seek the same—but it can also distract you from seeing what's right under your nose. When you're feeling envious, this card suggests you should take a moment to look at your own love life more closely. Have you been overlooking the riches you already have in your relationships?

The card can also speak to a desire for independence, however. Your time and energy are real physical resources and you only have so much. You do not need to share every second and every ounce of your strength with other people, even when you're in a relationship with them. Ask to lean on someone else for a change, instead of letting people always lean on you. Identify how much of yourself you really want to share and stick to that.

The Card Reversed

The Four of Pentacles reversed takes the concept of jealousy to the next level—that of greed. It's a clear warning about learning to be happy with what you have as opposed to always wanting more. That applies emotionally, yes, but as a Pentacles card, this particularly applies to the real world. Have you been demanding too much of your partner? Do you expect friends and family to drop everything when you call? Is that healthy? What advice would you give someone else if they asked you how to stop treating people that way?

Another interesting aspect of the card is that of hoarding. Specifically, it's talking about hoarding your time and space and keeping it to yourself and the person you care about most. The card treats this as almost physical like you were hiding away jewels. And that's exactly how it works. You need to keep a few magic moments just for yourself and your special someone. Date nights. Private jokes. Little messages you leave for each other. These are small gestures, but they are worth their weight in gold, so store them up!

Affirmation

True wealth is measured in love. I am rich beyond imagining.

Five of Pentacles

Tough times come around, whether we like it or not. Sometimes these are small hurdles but at other times we feel like the bottom has fallen out of our world. Tough as they are, we can still learn something from experiences like this. The Five of Pentacles hold the key.

Common Portrayal

Two figures stumble through the snow. Behind them, five pentacles appear in the stained glass window of a church.

The Card Upright

The Five of Pentacles brings a message of hope at a time when you most need it. The card is focused on loss—a real loss that you can feel in your day-to-day life. This can be something as small as an argument with a roommate or as serious as a breakup or death. Whatever the case, it affects your relationships in a real and measurable way. But the Five of Pentacles reminds you that it is a temporary state of affairs. The Tarot doesn't often advise you to simply ignore something, but there are very rare occasions when you should do exactly that.

Some losses are so profound that dwelling on them can be harmful to you. They undermine your very faith in your ability to have meaningful relationships or even find love. At times like that, you need to cultivate indifference and a detached mindset. Only when you feel more secure should you attempt to deal with the problem—reach out to your ex, makeup with your friend, and process the loss. And even this detached mindset must be temporary as well, a moment to catch your breath before re-engaging with your life and your relationships.

The Card Reversed

Reversed, the Five of Pentacles speaks t0 your personal perceptions of your relationships and love life. It asks you how you feel about the state of affairs you're in. Traditionally, this card spoke of being wealthy or poor—in the context of your relationships, it's telling you to take stock.

How happy are you? What is missing? What more can you be giving to those you care about? The card doesn't care what the answers are, only that you ask the questions. You will judge your answers yourself.

The card also poses the question: *Is it worth it?* You'll be presented with all manner of temptations in your love life, physical as well as emotional. When you're considering giving in to one of these temptations, remember the message of the Five of Pentacles reversed. Are you wealthy enough in love as it is? Are you being greedy? What might you stand to lose if you go through with this?

Affirmation

Pain is fleeting. Love is eternal.

Six of Pentacles

♥

Pay it forward. When you're winning, don't hog all the glory. Spread some of that love around and you'll find it reflected back at you. We're communal creatures and just one of us can make a difference for us all. The Six of Pentacles know just how to make that happen.

Common Portrayal

A well-dressed individual gives alms to beggars. Six pentacles float above them.

The Card Upright

The Six of Pentacles is all about generosity. Specifically, it's about being generous with your time and energy—your physical presence—for those you care about. It's the card of giving, giving, and giving some more. As a solution to questions in your relationship and love life, it's a surprisingly simple approach. Give more. Be generous with yourself. Be there for the ones you care about. This will add deep strength to your relationships. Being there emotionally is one thing. Actually, pitching up in person sends a message on a whole other level.

Similarly, the Six of Pentacles is a reminder that it's okay to be on the receiving end of generosity as well. Some people are happy to share but feel awkward or embarrassed when someone wants to help them out or give them a gift. This is a natural response, but you should try to move past it in your relationships. Show that you see and appreciate the other person's gesture. They care about you and want to see that you understand that. Being open to their generosity is the best way to do that.

The Card Reversed

The Six of Pentacles reversed looks inwards and asks whether you're being generous enough with yourself. As the Tarot is fond of saying, your first relationship is the one you have with yourself, and so the one you must nurture above all others. In order to be healthy and happy in love, you must make real space for yourself. Treat yourself.

Indulge yourself. This kind of self-care helps keep you positive and engaged in your relationships.

Secondly, the reversed version of the card is a warning against giving too much of your own time and space to the people around you. It's not just about making time for yourself—this is a frequent message in the Tarot—but more about setting boundaries in your relationships. Make sure the people close to you know how much you're willing to give and where you draw the line—and make sure you know that about them as well. Healthy communication and clear boundaries make for strong relationships.

Affirmation

All I have, I give. All I have is love.

Seven of Pentacles

❤

It's great when a plan comes together. Everything falls into place just as you intended, and your love life is nice and smooth. But the operative word here is *plan*—all of this didn't happen by accident and the Seven of Pentacles will make sure you're on point.

Common Portrayal

A tired figure rests on their gardening hoe, gazing at their plants. The plant bears seven pentacles as fruit.

The Card Upright

The Seven of Pentacles is focused on helping you find real happiness in your relationships by asking you to think ahead and carefully assess your needs. If you have an honest understanding of what you want in your love life, you can make concrete plans on how to achieve it. These can be personal goals such as getting fit, starting dating again, or speaking up for yourself when you need to. But these goals can also include others—finding a partner, starting a family, choosing a home.

What matters is that you approach your relationship goals with clear intent. Relationships don't happen in a vacuum or fantasy. They happen in the real world. Ask yourself what would need to change for you to feel happier about your love life. Can you name what it is? This practical approach to your relationships will help you see clearly how your needs will interact with the real world. From there, you can start to shape your love life to meet those needs.

The Card Reversed

The Seven of Pentacles reversed takes a different perspective on the matter of planning out your relationship goals. Instead, it asks whether you've taken on too many goals and are trying to accomplish too much at once. Are you juggling dating, time with friends, family responsibilities, a career, and some alleged free time all at once? If you're always planning your next move, how can you enjoy where you are and who you're with right now?

On an even stronger note, the card also raises the question of when have you had enough. Part of setting out clear goals and expectations in your relationships is also knowing when to walk away. You cannot pour your heart and soul into something that has no life left in it. If this card speaks strongly to you, ask yourself whether there are aspects in your relationships that are upsetting you or proving problematic. What would it take to fix this problem? Is walking away a solution?

Affirmation

This is the road to happiness. I made it myself.

Eight of Pentacles

♥

If at first you don't succeed, or so the saying goes. And there's some truth to that—perseverance has its value. When taking this approach to relationships, you have to keep consent foremost in mind. With the Eight of Pentacles, you're sure to succeed.

Common Portrayal

A figure works carefully on a pentacle with tools. Seven others lie or hang nearby.

The Card Upright

Perseverance is at the heart of the Eight of Pentacles, but that's always a tricky element in relationships. When you've been turned down, the urge to take another shot can be strong—but should you always just take no for an answer? In most cases, yes, you should, but people can change their minds over time. Ask yourself how you would know whether some might be open to your advances. Is there a chance you might make them uncomfortable? Is it worth the risk of upsetting them?

And here we come to the true message of the card. Each of those questions shows a level of internal perseverance, a determination to reach a respectful decision. Being determined to treat your loved ones better is a powerful skill in all relationships. It means you're continually trying to be a better friend, a better partner, a better spouse. That internal perseverance ends up making a difference in the real world, a difference in your life and the lives of your loved ones.

The Card Reversed

The Eight of Pentacles reversed looks at the concept of perseverance taken to an extreme. And here we do see warnings against ignoring your partner's boundaries or acting without consent in your love life. But there's also an internal perspective, where the card is asking you whether you need to dial it back a little. The quest for internal perfection or the perfect relationship can have knock-on effects on your love life. If you're pouring all your energies into being the perfect partner, are you maybe neglecting your friends and family? Or vice versa?

This cuts both ways. As a good friend, partner, or spouse, you're naturally motivated to help those you care about become the best versions of themselves. You support their hobbies, their sporting interests, and their careers. But you can take this supporting role too far, particularly where it's to your detriment. The people who care about you will understand this. If they don't, they're not really the people who care about you, are they?

Affirmation

I am my own challenger. I am my own healer.

Nine of Pentacles

♥

True happiness is so close you can almost taste it. Your relationships are all fulfilling, your love life is purring along nicely, and you're on top of the world. So why do you feel like something's not right? The Nine of Pentacles will help you figure it out.

Common Portrayal

A woman stands in a bountiful garden, dressed in fine robes. Nine pentacles hang like fruit from the bushes in the garden.

The Card Upright

The Nine of Pentacles wants you to enjoy life. Yes, it's normal to feel unsure and uncomfortable with advice like this, particularly if you're struggling to find answers or are confused about your relationships. But the card wants you to enjoy yourself anyway. What's more, it's asking you to take a close look at your life and your relationships and *find* things to be happy about, even if you don't see them at first. The card is a call to remember how fortunate you are, even when you don't feel it.

Having people you can reach out to—friends, family, and loved ones—is a remarkable luxury and we can often overlook just how special it is to have people close to you to lean on during the hard times in life. Even when your love life isn't going quite how you'd like, there are still things to be hopeful about. Take a moment to look back at the last few months of your life and see how far you have come. Can you see ways you can help others in the same manner?

The Card Reversed

When reversed, the Nine of Pentacles wants you to look inside and see the value that's there. While the upright card asks you to appreciate the bounty in your love life, the reversed card wants you to see that same worth in yourself. It's the Tarot's eternal message of self-love and it's asking you to understand that you're deserving of love, that you will find happiness, and that you're the kind of person that others want to be with in life and in love.

If you're struggling to see this, ask yourself what your friends and family would say about you if they were asked. How would they describe you? If you're honest with yourself and have been treating your loved ones well, you'll have to admit that they'd talk about you in loving and appreciative terms. So why can't you see yourself that way? What would need to happen for you to be able to appreciate yourself as your loved ones do? What's stopping that from happening?

Affirmation

I see my worth. It is without limit.

Ten of Pentacles

♥

When your love life is fulfilling and your friends and family are gathered around you in support, it can feel like there's nothing you can't accomplish. Well, that's true—there isn't. You have it within you to achieve all you have dreamed of. The Ten of Pentacles has great things in store for you.

Common Portrayal

A figure sits in the courtyard of a luxurious home, his family and pets around him. Ten pentacles adorn the scene.

The Card Upright

The Ten of Pentacles deals with security and happiness in your love life and asks how you will make the most of that to improve the lives of those around you. You may not have actually achieved everything you want in your relationships but the card suggests looking at your accomplishments—dealing with heartbreak, finding a new partner, being there for your friends and family, setting boundaries for yourself in relationships—and then figuring out how you can pour those successes back into the lives of those you care about.

Even when you're struggling, you can find the strength to be there for your loved ones. It may only be in small ways, but they will notice, and this can only deepen the bond between you. In a relationship, you can be the strong one for your partner when they're in times of crisis. You can support your friends and family when they have no one else to turn to. And you can be there for your loved ones in small ways as well, with little gestures of kindness and love. Each one counts.

The Card Reversed

The Ten of Pentacles reversed questions the value of happiness and stability itself. It asks you to account for what you're doing in your love life, and your relationship. The card takes no account of right or wrong—it doesn't care if you're cheating on your spouse or lying to your children or secretly helping a sick relative—it just cares that *you* understand what you're doing, and why. Are you fully aware of the reasons for and consequences of your actions where your loved ones are concerned? If not, clearly, you must spend the necessary time coming to an understanding of where you're headed.

But that's only part of the card's message because once you have a proper understanding of your behavior, the Ten of Pentacles reversed asks you whether it's worth it. Do you really need what you're chasing? If you get it (a lover, a marriage, a friend), will it make you happier than you are now? If so, why? What is at the root of your desire to improve your love life? As before, the reversed card doesn't care what you answer. Only that you do.

Affirmation

This is my wealth. This is my joy.

Page of Pentacles

♥

Getting back out into the world is a challenging and exciting time. You've been away, recharging your batteries, and now you're ready to go. How much will things have changed while you were away? The Page of Pentacles will explain everything.

Common Portrayal

A page holds a single pentacle aloft. Flowers bloom all around.

The Card Upright

The Page of Pentacles is all about engaging (or re-engaging) with the world. You can only hide away for so long nursing your wounds. Sooner or later, you must get back out there. Begin dating again. Dare to trust. Open up to people. Attend awkward social events. Whatever you choose, one thing remains unchanged—you can't have a relationship if you don't meet people. You may want to remain single right now, and that's fine, but if not, the card is pretty clear on what you have to do.

To follow the Page's example as a source of fresh ideas, you should also make sure that at least some of your approaches are new. If you've always chosen dates through a dating app, try meeting someone in person (or vice versa!). If you turn down all invitations to parties, try attending one for a change. Mix up the structure and pattern of your love life and you'll find the results refreshing and exciting.

The Card Reversed

Reversed, the Page of Pentacles wants you to meet someone else before you become socially active again. Yourself. We all go through changes and the Page of Pentacles reversed is a call to reacquaint yourself with who you are before you begin sharing yourself with friends and loved ones again. You might be the same person but isn't it worth spending some time alone with yourself to be sure? As an inquisitive person, what questions might you ask yourself?

The card also asks you to look back at your previous experiences in relationships before considering starting a new one or looking for a new one. Do you have a strong idea about what went wrong in failed relationships in the past? Or what went right in the ones that worked for you? Are there things you need to change about your behavior or boundaries you need to set for others? What advice would you give your younger self about starting a new relationship?

Affirmation

I shape my world. I build it with love.

Knight of Pentacles

♥

There are two ways to deal with any problem—the right way and the wrong way—and you're only interested in one of those. You know what you want, and you know exactly how to get there. The Knight of Pentacles approves!

Common Portrayal

An armored knight sits atop a stationary horse. He holds a pentacle in one hand.

The Card Upright

The Knight of Pentacles isn't the most exciting card, but its advice always delivers results. Always. The card is a call to be methodical and steady in your approach to your love life—at least where your current questions are concerned. This could range from something as simple as finding out what your special someone's favorite food is so you can surprise them with a meal, to devising a highly complex scoring system to keep track of and rate your dates. Whatever the case, the Knight's advice is not to take a haphazard approach to your relationships. Be determined.

The card is also a reminder not to mess with a good thing. As disheartening as it may be, there's more to romance than wild excitement and sometimes a relationship that seems predictable and unadventurous can nevertheless be wholesome, loving, and enduring. Similarly, if you have found that you have certain requirements in a partner, you shouldn't change that just because others pressure you to. So long as you respect yourself and others, it's okay to impose criteria on those you allow into your love life. You'd be happy to date anyone otherwise, and that's clearly not how the world works.

The Card Reversed

The Knight of Pentacles reversed is a call to impose some discipline on yourself. If this card speaks strongly to you, you might ask yourself if you've been a little out of control recently, acting irresponsibly, or otherwise behaving unaccountably. Yes, life is more fun that way, for a while at least, but your love life can only take so much chaos before it starts to come apart at the seams. So, try reining in your wilder tendencies a little and see how those around you respond. If they seem happier, do you even need to ask yourself why?

Somewhat perversely, the reversed version of the card also cautions against being too cautious. If you've been isolating yourself and shutting out the world, then clearly it would be better to spend time with people. The point of the reversed card is balance, that old favorite of the Tarot. If you're leaning too far one way or the other, your relationships will be unnecessarily unruly or staid, as the case may be. Walk the golden path between the two.

Affirmation

A journey contains countless steps. I will count each one.

Queen of Pentacles

♥

Your priorities are simple. There's you and your family, and then there's everyone else. That doesn't mean you can't have a love life and meaningful and lasting relationships with people. So long as they understand your priorities. The Queen of Pentacles knows exactly what you mean.

Common Portrayal

A queen sits on her throne, cradling a pentacle. Nearby, a rabbit runs past.

The Card Upright

The Queen of Pentacles stands for all those who build their lives around their families. She recognizes the challenges this brings. Looking for and finding—never mind sustaining—a love life when you have a full-time family is hard. You're making countless sacrifices on all sides in order to just *have* both sides. At times, it feels like you're just getting everything wrong. The Queen of Pentacles is here to tell you not to be too hard on yourself. This is just the shape relationships take when you bend them around a family. If you manage to juggle both, you should be proud of yourself, not critical.

You can carry that same energy into the relationship itself. You and your partner form a family as well—one that only includes the two of you. You should protect that as well, nurture it, and help it grow. Those you care about will respect that, and that includes your regular family. This brings you happiness in all aspects of your relationships, allowing you to share that positive energy back in turn.

The Card Reversed

The Queen of Pentacles reversed asks you to turn that nurturing energy inwards. Rather than concerning yourself with families, relationships, and lovers, the card asks you to think of yourself as a family of one. Spending time caring for yourself, seeing to your own needs, hobbies, interests—whatever you desire—makes you a more rounded, more contented person, more able to find love and long-lasting happiness.

The card reversed can also point to an imbalance in how you're juggling the various competing demands on your time. Are you spending too much time and energy on your love life, to the detriment of friends and family? Have you left a lover hanging because you wanted to spend time with your friends? The card suggests correcting these imbalances before they spiral out of control. As always, balance is the key to happy relationships.

Affirmation

Love begins here. This is its home.

King of Pentacles

There's only one thing better than having everything you ever wanted, and that's giving it away. As you enrich the lives of those around you, so is yours in turn enriched. There's nothing so valuable that its value can't be increased by sharing it. So says the King of Pentacles.

Common Portrayal

A king sits on his throne, his robes decorated with grapes and vines. He holds a scepter in one hand and a pentacle in the other.

The Card Upright

The King of Pentacles teaches you that giving your time and energy to those you care about will bring you true happiness in love and your relationships. While other cards caution against giving up too much of yourself, the King of Pentacles presumes you're in a position to make use of its advice. Like all powerful cards in the Tarot, it demands things of you. It pushes you to be a better version of yourself in order to achieve the happiness you're looking for.

The card is asking you to be sure you understand your own needs, as they manifest in the real world, not in the abstract. Do you have clear boundaries? Are you open and honest with yourself and others? This card calls on you to put all you have learned about love and relationships into practice, purely so you have the wisdom and experience to share with those you care about. There's an altruism there that can be very fulfilling, as the truest expression of love—the act of giving something precious. Yourself.

The Card Reversed

The King of Pentacles reversed is a humbling card but one whose lesson we all must draw on from time to time. It tells us that even when our love life is perfect, our relationships harmonious, and our friendships invigorating, we are not immune to hardship. We can fall and sometimes we fall hard. At times like that, our shame can lead us to hide away when we should be reaching out to those close to us. The King of Pentacles reversed is a reminder to do just that.

If you feel like you had the perfect marriage or the best partner or the coolest friends and now it's all gone, the last thing you want to do is face up to how much you've lost. You might even be embarrassed to be seen by those you care about. The King of Pentacles reversed also wants to remind you that love doesn't work like that. The people who really love you *want* to be there for you when you're down. It's why they're there. After all, wouldn't you do the same for the people you love?

Affirmation

My journey ends where it began. With love.

Chapter 5:
Suggested spreads

♥

A "Tarot spread" is the way you arrange the cards when you are doing a reading, and honestly, any spread you are comfortable with will work. There is no right or wrong way to do it. Organized spreads assign different aspects of your question to different cards. For example, a three-card layout can represent you, your partner, and the status of your relationship. You'd then read the card that goes in each spot for a more complete answer.

The Tarot is a system of digging deep into your issues rather than a simple question and a simple answer. Imagine sitting at a coffee shop for a long while with your best friend, really mulling over a particular issue you are facing. The Tarot is that best friend.

For example, instead of asking "when will I meet my soul mate?" the Tarot does it better by breaking down all aspects of your question:

- What do I need to do to prepare for this person to be in my life?

- What will this person be like? What am I looking for?

- What will our relationship together be like?

Tarot spreads help you break down your question into those various elements so you are digging deeper into your issue. You use multiple cards, with each card representing a different part of your question.

You can see why this is not a system that does well with "yes" or "no" questions. Take care to frame your questions so that it doesn't require a "yes" or a "no." Instead of asking "does he like me?" ask "how does he feel about me?" and enjoy the deeper answer you get from it.

If you are intent on getting the answer to a yes/no question, there are guides you can find online where you can manipulate your cards to work that way (these cards mean a "yes," and these cards mean a "no.") I personally haven't had much luck with doing it that way. I always feel that even though I am going for a simple yes or no, the card I draw is always trying to tell me more than that. The imagery or meaning relates in some way and gets my curiosity going. I end up doing a full reading in the end anyway!

There are other divination tools out there that are better suited to yes/no questions. An easy one to hunt down is a pendulum board. You can find them cheap online or in your local metaphysical shop, or you can make one easily enough. It's a circle with yes, no, maybe, and rephrase your question written around it. It's kind of like using a magic 8 ball, honestly. You dangle a necklace (or they make pendulums to match your pendulum board) over the board and hold it as still as possible. The pendulum will naturally swing left and right, or up and down, indicating the answer to our question.

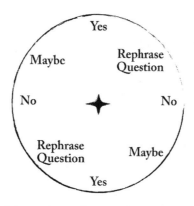

Back to the Tarot, have fun exploring layouts for your different questions, and try not to over-complicate things by doing too intricately involved spreads. I have seen some spreads that use more than twenty cards, which I think would be overwhelming! The biggest one I have included in this book is ten cards. There are infinitely more ideas you can find online too. I have a couple of spreads I regularly use for most of my readings, and then I play with a few others as needed. Find your niche and roll with it.

(A note to my audiobook listeners: I will include a pdf of these layouts for you to reference.)

Suggested spreads for love questions:

The Check-In Spread – 1 Card

This is a quick look at how things are going. You can pull a card daily for your relationship to check in.

Card 1: How is your relationship right now?

The Quick Look Spread – 3 Cards

Here's another quick look at your relationship, but this one gives more information than the single-card layout.

Card 1: You

Card 2: Your partner

Card 3: The state of the relationship

The Status of Things Spread — 6 Cards

This one answers the infamous "where is this relationship going" question.

Card 1: You

Card 2: Your partner

Card 3: How are you connected to each other?

Card 4: How strong is your relationship?

Card 5: How are you weak as partners?

Card 6: Outcome of the relationship

The "Let it Go" Spread – 6 Cards

Whether it's for a fight you've had with your significant other that you need to move past or an ex you are trying to get over, there's lots of uses for this "Let it Go" spread regarding your relationship.

Card 1: What I'm feeling right now.

Card 2: Why am I feeling this way?

Card 3: Why can't I move past it?

Card 4: How can I let it go?

Card 5: What's ahead for me if I can let it go?

Card 6: What's the life lesson in this?

The "Help Me Understand" Spread – 7 Cards

This is a great spread to help you understand miscommunications and disagreements you may be having with your partner.

Card 1: The person you are asking about

Card 2, 3 and 4: Why are they doing it? Or what are the assumptions I am making about it?

Card 5 and 6: What's going on behind the scenes that I don't know about?

Card 7: The real reason this is happening.

Tip: I don't always randomly deal out card #1 (the one that represents your partner) in this spread. If a particular card fits your person to a "T" then use it here. For example, if your boyfriend reminds you of the emperor card, then put the emperor card in this spot to clarify your reading. If you don't have a card that fits, then deal out card #1 randomly from your deck.

The "I'm Ready for My Soulmate" Spread – 10 Cards

Are you ready for Mr. or Ms. Right to finally show up in your life? Ask your Tarot cards about it!

Card 1: Why haven't I found them yet?

Card 2: What can I do about it?

Card 3: How can I speed things up?

Card 4: How will I find them?

Card 5: How will I know it's them?

Card 6: When will I find them?

Card 7: What do I need to know about the situation?

Card 8: What will my first impression be?

Card 9: What will bind us together?

Card 10: What does our future hold together?

Conclusion: It's not just about the cups.

♥

Most people think love readings are all about the Lovers, or the Suit of Cups, but as you can see, really any card in your deck can be applied to what's happening in your relationship right now. So many story lines are depicted in these brilliant cards that can be matched together in infinite ways to convey guidance on whatever you are facing. It's no wonder they have been around for hundreds of years, and still draw our curiosity and imagination.

Having been in the Tarot community for as many years as I have at this point, I see lots of people that wrestle with big questions, trying so hard to divine meanings from their cards and not having luck. I am here to say that we are all intuitive beings with the ability to do this baked right into us. It takes practice in this noisy world to get quiet, find the balance between your head and your heart, and learn to tune into yourself. There is ample wisdom to be found there, and I want you to be able to access it.

I hope this book has helped clear the way, with some organization over how you set up and carry out your readings. I hope card meanings make more sense to you when applied to a love reading. I hope the way forward with whatever you face is clearer, and you feel less alone in your struggles. Have patience with yourself as you learn. It is impossible to learn everything there is to know about the Tarot, but you can reach a point where you know enough to feel more confident and get what you need from it more often than not.

To wrap things up, I just want to say I am proud of you. It takes courage to put yourself out there and to risk your heart. The rewards when you find your match make it all worth it, but it can be a painful process, kissing a few frogs to find your prince (or princess!) I hope this guidebook helps give you another tool to use as you find your way through this life journey, and that your favorite Tarot deck makes a little more sense than it did before. Best of luck as you work through it. You've got this!

Thanks for purchasing The Tarot Book of Love. I really hope you enjoyed it. As an author, I would appreciate any feedback you have. Please use the following link to tell me your thoughts through a review. Thank you!

Link to Review: bit.ly/TBOLReview
(NOTE: The link is case sensitive.)